Michael Cassidy's Window on the Word

compiled by David Hewetson

Prayers by
David Hewetson

AQUILA
PRESS

A book by Aquila Press

Published October 1997
Copyright © Michael Cassidy 1997

Scripture taken from the
HOLY BIBLE, NEW INTERNATIONAL VERSION
Copyright © 1973, 1978, 1984 by
International Bible Society

Attempts to identify the copyright owner of *The Cradle Way* were unsuccessful. We would like to include the appropriate acknowledgment in subsequent editions of this book.

Aquila Press
PO Box A287, Sydney South, NSW 1235

National Library of Australia
ISBN 1 875861 38 6

Cover art by Jenny Nisbet

Printed in Australia by Australian Print Group

Dedication

To David and Ann Hewetson, Mike and Jane
Woodall, and all in AE Australia, plus our many
friends in Wallabyland, I dedicate this volume with
gratitude and joy.

Preface

I must say I feel greatly indebted to David Hewetson, Mike Woodall and our African Enterprise Board and Staff for catching the vision of taking some of my newspaper articles from the past and editing them into this present form as a devotional volume. It is a wonderful illustration of the principle of multiplication whereby one takes one piece of work and makes it go double the distance.

The story of my *Window on the Word* column in some of the South African newspapers goes back to 1968. We were just starting out our ministry and were doing a youth mission in the southern suburbs of Cape Town. One day a notion seized me (I like to think it was the voice of the Spirit) that I should approach the editor of our local newspaper in Pietermaritzburg, where African Enterprise was and is headquartered, and ask him whether I could do a regular religious column in his newspaper. I was a cheeky young fellow and just getting started. Yet this did not throw the editor and to my total astonishment he replied: 'I have been thinking for some time of something like this and would like to do it. When would you like to start? How long do you want it to be? And where would you like it to be placed in the paper?' I was completely taken aback, but singing doxologies in my heart nevertheless. I said to him: 'Well, sir, I would like to start right away. I suggest about 600 words. And how about on the Editorial page?' With the benevolent smile of a long-experienced newspaper hand, now disarmed and undone by this naive novice, he looked across his desk at me and said: 'Well, so be it. Let's start next Saturday!'

And so it was that my *Window on the Word* column was born in 1968. I wrote it weekly for 15 to 18 years in *The Natal Witness* in Pietermaritzburg. In due time it was used in other newspapers such as *The Star* in Johannesburg and *The Cape Argus* in Cape Town. Some of the articles even went up to a Christian newspaper in Kenya. A few found their way into an Inter-Varsity Evangelistic booklet.

I have continued to write for that newspaper ever since, although now I share the column with five or six other regular writers. But I have always felt I owed much more to this column than it ever owed to me. The fact was that it required of me to submit to the discipline once a week of doing a concise article and trying to couch it in terms which the ordinary lay person would understand and receive. To keep it alive I also adopted the philosophy of letting it be semi-autobiographical, in the sense that I could only sustain a column long term if I wrote out of my own experience as to where I was at the moment of writing. So the column tended to follow what was happening around me in South Africa or in the world or in my own heart. I think that gave it some life, vitality and authenticity.

And now my good and dear Christian friends in Wallabyland (who now and then are beastly to the Springboks) have taken up the notion of editing some of these articles into a modified and slightly abbreviated form for this present volume. I feel touched and humbled by the feeling they have that these articles could be of further use and blessing to the Christian public. I certainly trust with all my heart that this will be the case.

I want to express very special gratitude to David Hewetson who did the editing work and who has painstakingly assembled the material in its present form. Mike Woodall has been very gracious to pursue his vision for this volume and I thank him too with all my heart. And then there is Heather Valentine and the Aussie office who have typed and retyped some of the reworked articles in this present form. Beyond that I want to thank my dear secretary, Mrs Colleen Smith, who typed most of these articles in the first instance and continues to do this kind of work for me on a regular basis. I owe her the world for all this help all down the years. Another special colleague is Mrs Lois Stephenson who has also over the years helped with my column and in this instance has contributed some further editing and correcting of the galley proofs.

I know that in so many ways I could not have this kind of ministry opportunity but for the wonderful and godly help of many precious brothers and sisters both there in Australia and here in South Africa. To all of these, and above all to the Lord who inspires us all with His Love, I express my loving gratitude and appreciation.

May you, the reader, be blessed as you are exposed to these pages.

Michael Cassidy
Pietermaritzburg
August 1997

Introduction

Sifting through Michael Cassidy's articles – there were hundreds of them – was a task I enjoyed very much. Michael has the preacher's ear for picking up stories with meaning. As a stout defender of the faith he is also tough-minded enough to take on widely held misconceptions and misapprehensions about Christianity. As a true-hearted evangelist he is always at the ready to present Christ and the Gospel in a winning way. Michael is a great traveller and in some articles we are in Africa, perhaps at work with African Enterprise teams, sometimes we are out in the wider world, but in all of them our hearts and minds are directed towards God. For me it was fun to 'eavesdrop' on the agile Cassidy mind and I trust you will find it helpful too.

Some of the stories in this book will make you chuckle, some will make you very thoughtful and – with the attached Bible passages – we hope your heart and mind will fasten on some important spiritual truth. I have taken the liberty of adding short prayers to the articles so that you can speak with the Lord about what you have just read. So welcome to Michael Cassidy's *Window on the Word*.

David Hewetson
International Chairman, African Enterprise

Discover your potential

This is the word that came to Jeremiah from the Lord: 'Go down to the potter's house, and there I will give you my message.' So I went down to the potter's house, and I saw him working at the wheel. But the pot he was shaping from the clay was marred in his hands; so the potter formed it into another pot, shaping it as seemed best to him.

Then the word of the Lord came to me: 'O house of Israel, can I not do with you as this potter does?' declares the Lord. 'Like the clay in the hand of the potter, so are you in my hand, O house of Israel.'

(Jeremiah 18:1–6)

●●●

In the back streets of Cairo I once watched an old-fashioned potter at work. He took and turned an amorphous blob of clay into a finished form of genuine beauty. He obviously knew exactly what he wanted to do. He saw the potential hidden in each blob of clay. Occasionally he also took up a dud piece of pottery, broke it and moistened it until it was ready to re-fashion. It reminded me of the words of Jeremiah.

Our God is the God of potentialities. He sees in every person their hidden possibilities and he longs for each one to become yielding and flexible in his hand, to be re-fashioned to bring out their real potential.

When God asked Amos in the Old Testament to be a prophet he protested that he was nothing of the sort – he was a farmer. But God saw his potential and sent him off to issue powerful warnings to the nation.

When Jesus met Simon the fisherman he re-named him 'Rock' (Peter) because behind Peter's impulsive and unpredictable surface Jesus saw a strong and reliable leader. Though, like Amos, Peter had his moments of self-doubt, he was now in the Divine Potter's hands and a new and beautiful vessel was in the making.

Prayer:
O God, I put myself into your strong and loving hands. Make me and re-make me till I am what you want me to be. Bring out in me a beauty that I cannot see but which is plainly visible to you. For Jesus' sake. Amen.

Putting things back
2000 years

All the believers were one in heart and mind. No-one claimed that any of his possessions was his own, but they shared everything they had. With great power the apostles continued to testify to the resurrection of the Lord Jesus, and much grace was upon them all. There were no needy persons among them. For from time to time those who owned lands or houses sold them, brought the money from the sales and put it at the apostles' feet, and it was distributed to anyone as he had need.

(Acts 4:32–35)

●●●

An American church leader once took a bold initiative in a certain Californian city. Some locals were horrified: 'he has set the church back fifty years'!

He replied: 'No, I don't want to set the church back fifty years; I want to set it back 2000 years.'

Society today demands that we look only to the future, to 'progress'. But sometimes it is also necessary for Christians to look back to the early church. Its members were by no means perfect but they got some things so right that we must never forget them or lose them.

The *people*: They were a diverse and varied lot. Peter – bluff, brash and impulsive; John – shy, retiring and sensitive; Philip – quick to believe; Thomas – slow to believe. But they all learned from Jesus how to make room for one another and become a team that could begin to win the world for him.

The *power*: Nothing could stop them. Not persecution, not mockery, not even the might of the State. By the power of God's Spirit they took on all comers – it has been said of St Paul that wherever he went there was either riot or revival!

The *purpose*: They were like excited beggars telling other beggars where to find bread. They shared the Good News of Jesus and his salvation wherever and whenever they could. They were signposts to the lost, carers to the needy, messengers of hope to an anxious world.

Prayer:
Dear Lord, please continue to empower us with your Spirit so that we do not lose the joy and commitment that rightly belongs to your people in every age. Amen.

3

The once-wound clock

The hour has come for you to wake up from your slumber, because our salvation is nearer now than when we first believed. The night is nearly over; the day is almost here. So let us put aside the deeds of darkness and put on the armour of light.

(Romans 13:11–12)

●●●

Inscribed on a clock in the Botanic Gardens in Durban, South Africa are the following words:

The clock of life is wound but once:
And no man has the power to tell just when the hands will stop
– at late or early hour.
Now is the only time you own:
Live, love, toil with a will:
And place no faith in tomorrow, for the clock may then be still.

Eighty years from now even the youngest among us will be in eternity – most of us will get there a lot sooner.

I am increasingly conscious of the shortness of life. I often meditate on the fact that we have one opportunity in life. There will be no re-run, no second chances, no reincarnation. How important it is not to waste our opportunity!

The Psalmist asked God to teach him to 'number' his days so that he could be wise in the use of them. How wonderful to make the discovery that is stated so well in the Westminster Confession: that our chief end in life is 'to glorify God and enjoy him forever'.

Stop, look and listen. The greatest moment in your life is right now. 'Now is the accepted time. Today is the day of salvation'.

Prayer:
God, give us the wisdom to make the very most of life. The clock ticks on and we do not have unlimited time. Help us to use our years, months, weeks, days and even hours as wisely as possible. For Jesus' sake. Amen

4

Room in the suitcase

All Scripture is God-breathed and is useful for teaching, rebuking, correcting and training in righteousness, so that the man of God may be thoroughly equipped for every good work.
(2 Timothy 3:16–17)

●●●

I have gotten pretty used to packing my case before leaving for ministry overseas. If you are like me, you will always have problems finding room for everything you want to take.

I heard of a minister who was packing his case while a friend looked on with some amusement. When there seemed to be room for nothing else the minister looked up and said: 'I can still fit in a guide book, a lamp, a mirror, a telescope, a book of poems, a number of biographies, some old letters, a hymn book and a small library of nearly 30 volumes'.

He was, of course, talking about his Bible.

How sad that so many people deprive themselves of the riches found in the Bible. It can bring food to the pilgrim, guidance to the perplexed, comfort to the sorrowing, hope to the dying, strength to the weak, a rebuke to the indifferent. Abraham Lincoln once said of Scripture: 'It is the best gift God has given to man'.

Why is it so special?

As the verse above says the Bible is 'useful' for a number of reasons all of which train us to live, to equip us and make us into the sort of people we are meant be. God has 'breathed' into it so that, as no other book can, it brings spiritual life and vitality to the reader.

Don't leave it out of your suitcase.

Prayer:
Father, thank you for the Bible and for not leaving us to our own devices. Thank you for words which sometimes sting and unsettle us, but which always lead us into better and more joyful paths. For Jesus' sake. Amen.

5

Shock result

Then one of the elders asked me, 'These in white robes – who are they, and where did they come from?'
I answered, 'Sir, you know.'
And he said, 'These are they who have come out of the great tribulation; they have washed their robes and made them white in the blood of the Lamb. Therefore, 'they are before the throne of God and serve him day and night in his temple; and he who sits on the throne will spread his tent over them. Never again will they hunger; never again will they thirst. The sun will not beat upon them nor any scorching heat. For the Lamb at the centre of the throne will be their shepherd; he will lead them to springs of living water. And God will wipe away every tear from their eyes.'

(Revelation 7:13–17)

●●●

I saw a cartoon some time ago when the British Lions Rugby team was visiting South Africa: A Roman senator was walking past the Colosseum in second century Rome. He sees a huge billboard: 'SHOCK RESULT – Christians defeat Lions'. Today when we have one of our city-wide missions it all seems so much easier. The arena is booked, the programme is planned, the choirs assemble and the PA system is plugged in.

Those who come to the arena and respond to the message are not going to face lions. They will not be persecuted or lose their jobs or be physically assaulted. It is more likely that their profession of faith will be met with a yawn or an amused smile. Has it all become too easy? Is that where danger lurks for us?

Let history speak. The persecution of Christians in the first three centuries began with some foreboding signs, then sustained hostility until there was fierce and bloody cruelty. It was a war of extermination which was to end only when the Emperor Constantine had a remarkable change of heart in AD 313.

Unfortunately for those who were bent on eradicating Christianity, it had already taken root in a fairly wide area. But then nine great waves of persecution followed, each as brutal as can be imagined. The Christians were harassed and hammered but they stood their ground. They stayed true to Jesus Christ for their own sake, and for ours. And yes, the Christians did finally defeat the lions!

Perhaps by comparison what we are up against seems like pussy cats. But beware, their little claws can be sharp and poisonous.

Prayer:
O Lord, we thank you for those who did not love their lives so much they shrank from death, and also for those who today in many places are showing the same kind of courage and dedication. Please help us too to fight bravely under Christ's banner against all those things that diminish his glory. For his name's sake. Amen.

6

The power struggle

Come and see what God has done, how awesome his works on man's behalf! He turned the sea into dry land, they passed through the waters on foot – come, let us rejoice in him. He rules forever by his power, his eyes watch the nations – let not the rebellious rise up against him. Praise our God, O peoples, let the sound of his praise be heard; he has preserved our lives and kept our feet from slipping.

(Psalm 66:5–9)

•••

At 5.30 am on 16 July 1945 a light brighter than a dozen suns lit up the desert sands of New Mexico. A scientist watching began to weep: 'My God' he exclaimed, 'we have created hell'.

On that fateful day the world changed. Atomic weapons gave a new perspective to the international power struggle. Countries with the Bomb soon decided to limit its use for themselves and to discourage its production by others.

When we think of power struggles we think of armies and bombs and guns. We think of competing ideologies and philosophies, of political victory and defeat. But in many ways the ultimate struggle for control is locked within our own hearts and minds. For some it means getting to the top – Julius Caesar said 'I would rather be first at Brundisium than second at Rome'. Alexander the Great and Napoleon

Bonaparte were inwardly tortured by the lust to rule the world.

For others money is the measure of power. It 'talks' and others jump at the sound of its voice. Still others contend for social position, not only keeping up with the fabled Joneses but actually getting ahead of them.

But for all of us there is a more definitive power struggle. It is the fight between good and evil within us, between being genuine or phoney, generous or selfish, arrogant or humble. At this point the Christian view of power is utterly relevant. It tells us that ultimate power is not in guns and bombs, political parties or financial and social success. The Psalmist tells us power belongs to God. It is the power of love, the cleansing power that flows from the cross of Christ.

To win the power struggle we do not need to get stronger in our own strength and win our battles by personality power. We need to be honest enough to admit our great weakness, and learn to plug in by faith to the One from whom all goodness flows.

Prayer:
Lord of all might and power, move in us and exert your strength within us to overcome all those struggles that we can never overcome by our own strength. We praise you for the power that heals and helps, that forgives and invigorates. Amen.

What the bus driver said

'Has a nation ever changed its gods? (Yet they are not gods at all.) But my people have exchanged their Glory for worthless idols. Be appalled at this, O heavens, and shudder with great horror,' declares the Lord. 'My people have committed two sins: They have forsaken me, the spring of living water, and have dug their own cisterns, broken cisterns that cannot hold water.'

(Jeremiah 2:11–13)

● ● ●

A New York bus driver who had driven his bus along the same route for years made a radical decision. Fed up with the routine of the same streets and stops he collected his empty bus at the depot and drove it out of New York City heading for Florida. Several days later he was picked up by the police and when questioned, he said that his life had become so meaningless and empty that he wanted to make a protest. When he returned to New York he got a hero's welcome since most people in that big city could identify with him.

When life loses its significance, boredom sets in. The driver felt that he had become a non-person, a zero, and that he had to do something drastic to find even a scrap of purpose in life. Actually his protest was profoundly philosophical and he was not the only one in our century who let out a cry of pain.

The poet T. S. Eliot wrote 'we are the hollow men' and the novelist Ernest Hemingway wrote 'there is no remedy for anything in life. Death is a sovereign remedy for all misfortunes'. Being a man of his word he later took a gun and blew out his brains.

The Bible's diagnosis for this all-pervasive human sickness is very frank: 'all have turned away, there is no one who does good'. Our meaninglessness comes from our waywardness, our boredom comes from our self-centredness, our despair arises out of our ruptured relationship with God.

Although the Bible says that this disease is malignant, fatal and incurable, it celebrates the fact that God's cure for it is all-powerful. The forgiveness that he offers in Jesus Christ, the new life and hope that he engenders in us, is the best news the world has ever heard. Even our brave bus driver could see that and join with St Augustine when he said to God, 'you have made us for yourself and our hearts are restless until they find their rest in you'.

Prayer:
Lord, left to ourselves we are empty and unfulfilled. Without you, life is meaningless and full of despair. Help us to recognise that you are the Fountain of Life, the source of all joy and peace, and that without you, we are running up a dead end street. We ask this in Jesus' name. Amen.

Time flies; we fly

The Eternal shepherds me, I lack for nothing; he makes me lie in meadows green, he leads me to refreshing streams, he revives life in me. He guides me by true paths, as he himself is true. My road may run through a glen of gloom, but I fear no harm, for thou art beside me; thy club, thy staff - they give me courage. Thou art my host, spreading a feast for me, while my foes have to look on! Thou hast poured oil upon my head, my cup is brimming over; yes, and all through my life Goodness and Kindness wait on me, the Eternal's guest within his household evermore.

(Psalm 23 Moffat translation)

●●●

I think I must have been born on the run because I find it so hard to slow down. But then I was also born into the mid-20th century and perhaps all I did was to catch a 20th century disease. Have you got it too? Did you catch it from me or did I catch it from you? Perhaps we caught it from each other!

Modern man finds the throttle stuck at full speed. In anguish he laments the fact that 'time flies'. But actually the real problem is not time, it is us and the way we use our time. No, time does not fly, *we* do. Time is not lost, *we* are. We waste it, or kill it or cram it so full of activity that there is no space left for the most important things in life.

As a prescription try this Chinese version of Psalm 23:

The Lord is my pacemaker, I shall not rush. He makes me stop for quiet intervals. He provides me with the images of stillness which restore my serenity. He leads me in ways of efficiency through calmness of mind, and his guidance is peace. Even though I have much to do I will not fret, for his presence is here. He gives refreshment and renewal in the midst of my activity, he anoints my mind with the oil of tranquillity, and my cup of joyous energy overflows. Surely harmony and effectiveness shall rule over my house, and I shall walk in the Lord's peace until I live in his house forever.

Prayer:

Slow me down, Lord. Ease the pounding of my heart and quieten my racing mind. Give me the vision of eternity to steady my pace and amid the frenzy of the day, give me the tranquillity of the everlasting hills. Let me go slow enough to see a flower, pat a dog, chat with a friend and read a few lines from a good book. Remind me again of those three years in which your Son gave us an enduring example in the use of time. For his name's sake. Amen.

9

The flight of faith

For what I received I passed on to you as of first importance: that Christ died for our sins according to the Scriptures, that he was buried, that he was raised on the third day according to the Scriptures, and that he appeared to Peter, and then to the Twelve. After that, he appeared to more than five hundred of the brothers at the same time, most of whom are still living, though some have fallen asleep. Then he appeared to James, then to all the apostles, and last of all he appeared to me also, as to one abnormally born.

(1 Corinthians 15:3–8)

●●●

Flying sometimes reminds me of the dynamics of faith. This modern miracle of travelling at speed over hundreds of miles and over whole nations and mighty oceans was once thought utterly impossible. Some people today think that in this sceptical scientific age, faith is also impossible. Hear then the parable of the aeroplane.

If I want to get from Durban to Johannesburg at 500 kilometres an hour there is no point in committing myself to my battered old VW. I need something like a Boeing 767. And faith alone is not enough, it needs to have the right focus. For Christian faith there is only one proper focus – Jesus Christ.

Christian faith is not blind optimism. It is sensible and reasonable. If I board an aeroplane which is unreliable or which is bound for a destination other than the one I want, then my 'faith' is simply foolishness. Christian faith is based on sound and rational evidence like Christ's fulfilment of the prophecies of the Old Testament, his peerless character, his monumental claims for himself, his unrivalled teaching, and his well documented resurrection from the dead.

If I had stood all day in the Durban airport and repeated over and over again 'I believe in aeroplanes' it would never have gotten me to Johannesburg.

To my convictions about the aircraft I had to add commitment to entering it and relying on it to get me to my destination. So it is with faith. To repeat the Apostle's Creed is useful. To be convinced that its statements are true is better still. But for real faith to be born in our hearts we must take the final step of commitment to Christ himself. It is then that our faith takes to the air and begins to carry us to our eternal destination.

Prayer:
O Lord, we thank you that the faith that you call us to have is not wishful thinking or mental gymnastics but based on truth and reality. We thank you for the sure foundation that you have given us in your Word so that, as we put our trust in you, our faith takes wing and carries us up into an eternal relationship with you. Amen.

Queen Victoria's question

Anyone who believes in the Son of God has this testimony in his heart. Anyone who does not believe God has made him out to be a liar, because he has not believed the testimony God has given about his Son. And this is the testimony: God has given us eternal life, and this life is in his Son. He who has the Son has life; he who does not have the Son of God, does not have life. I write these things to you who believe in the name of the Son of God so that you may know that you have eternal life.

(1 John 5:10–13)

●●●

After a service at St Paul's Cathedral, Queen Victoria asked a clergyman whether a person could be sure and certain that they had eternal life here and now. The minister replied: 'Your Majesty, such assurance is not possible'.

When this conversation was published in the Court News it caused a lot of discussion and some concern. Finally John Townsend, a humble minister in a remote English village wrote to the Queen and drew her attention to some Scripture passages which showed that a true believer can be certain of eternal life. In due course the Queen answered him with a letter of her own which said:

I have carefully and prayerfully read the portions of Scripture referred to. I now believe in the finished work of Christ for me and trust by God's grace to meet you in that Home of which He said 'I go to prepare a place for you'.

Signed:

Victoria.

After the Queen's important discovery she used to carry around a little booklet to give way to others. It was called *Safety, Certainty and Enjoyment*.

The assurance of salvation is the birthright of every Christian. Sadly there are some, like the clergyman at St Paul's, who feel that such a claim is presumption. But it is actually taking God at his word – a privilege and not a presumption. Verse after verse in the New Testament assures us that those who sincerely put their trust in Christ as Saviour and Lord are in his keeping for all time.

Prayer:

Lord Jesus, we gladly reaffirm our confidence in your many promises to us that we are yours forever and that even now we belong to you. We thank you that the sentence of 'not guilty' has already been handed down for us because of your death on the cross. Thank you for such an assurance. Amen.

Dimensions

'Since the beginning of the world the invisible attributes of God, eg his eternal power and divinity, have been plainly discernible through things which he has made and which are commonly seen and known, thus leaving these men without a rag of excuse. They knew all the time that there is a God, yet they refused to acknowledge him as such, or to thank him for what he is or does. Thus they became fatuous in their argumentations and plunged their silly minds still further in the dark'.

(Romans 1:19–21 – Philips Paraphrase)

●●●

A British scientist claimed that if every known star was reduced to a grain of sand we could cover the British Isles with a layer of sand 12 feet deep. Among those grains would be tiny Planet Earth. Populate that grain with billions of people and one of them would be you.

Travelling at 299,000 km per second, light takes 8 minutes to reach us from that minor star which we call the sun. But from the Andromeda Galaxy (the nearest to our Milky Way) light takes 800,000 years to reach us. And that is close – other light comes from much further out. Our little planet, travelling through space at 97,000 km per hour, is just the right distance from the sun. At double the distance we would freeze over, at half the distance we would fry.

So here we are, a dot in the middle of space racing round a dangerously hot star. What is it all about?

Did it all happen by chance, the result of some great cosmic accident? One biologist has observed that 'the probability of life originating from accident is comparable to the probability of the unabridged dictionary resulting from an explosion in a print shop'. Albert Einstein spoke of a 'peculiar religious feeling' among the best scientific minds of 'rapturous amazement at the harmony of natural law'.

The Bible says that 'the heavens declare the glory of God; the skies proclaim the work of his hands'. In wonder the Bible asks the important question, 'what is man that you are mindful of him?' And then in deepest thankfulness it celebrates the fact that the Maker of this vast universe once stepped on to our tiny grain of sand to rescue us from ourselves. To forget that fact is to miss the point of everything.

Prayer:
All this is too vast and too wonderful for us to comprehend. O Lord, we bow in worship before you at the majesty of your handiwork. We wonder at the loving concern with which you are so concerned for each and every one of us. We praise you for coming to identify with us and save us from our sins. Amen.

12

The broken things of life

If God is for us, who can be against us? He who did not spare his own Son, but gave him up for us all – how will he not also, along with him, graciously give us all things? Who will bring any charge against those whom God has chosen? It is God who justifies. Who is he that condemns? Christ Jesus, who died – more than that, who was raised to life – is at the right hand of God and is also interceding for us. Who shall separate us from the love of Christ?

(Romans 8: 31–35)

●●●

This word 'broken' seems to be a uniquely 20th century word. There are broken homes, broken promises, broken laws and broken lives. Modern people seem to be specialists in breaking things! And in consequence they are often broken themselves.

Yes, it is a modern malady, but right from the start Christianity concerned itself with the broken things of life. Thalasius, a Christian monk, founded the first asylum for the blind, Apollonius, a Christian merchant, set up the first free dispensary. And the first hospital on record was founded by Fabiola, a Christian lady.

Those early Christians got their mending model from Jesus himself. In a fragmented world he went about putting lives together again. To the weak and the ill he brought healing and wholeness; to the despised and rejected he brought respect and compassion; to the desperate and the guilt-ridden he brought hope and salvation; to an aimless world he gave meaning and direction. And he still does today.

Jesus sees the scattered bits and pieces of our lives and he gathers them together. He sees the fragmentation of our homes, the inner torment of our anxieties and he picks us up, cleans us up and sets us on our feet again. With our hand in his we find how true is the promise that, 'in all things God works for the good of those who love him who have been called according to his purpose'. Unlike Humpty Dumpty, God can put us together again.

Prayer:
O Jesus, Healer, Redeemer, Rescuer and Transformer, take hold of our brokenness and restore us to wholeness and health. Pick up the pieces, put them together and give us a new sense of direction and purpose. Amen.

13

Come and do some eavesdropping

The Apostle John said of himself and his book:
*This is the disciple who testifies to these things and
who wrote them down. We know that his testimony
is true. Jesus did many other things as well. If every
one of them were written down, I suppose that even
the whole world would not have room for the books
that would be written.*

(John 21:24–25)

•••

Let's listen in to some fascinating conversations.
Some of them are sad, some of them are glad and
some of them are red hot. And, unlike private
conversations, they were designed to be overheard.
So don't feel guilty about eavesdropping. But here is
a warning: some of the things that you will hear
might shake you a bit. It might provoke you and it
could possibly change you.

How do you do it? Simple. You get yourself a
good modern translation of the Bible and read it.
You will hear Jesus talking to theologians and civic
leaders. You will hear him have an intriguing
conversation with a woman with a sex problem. You
will hear him as he stands face to face with the
Roman governor of Jerusalem.

Never mind those old misconceptions that the
Bible is full of incomprehensible language and

unbelievable stories. Give the Bible a chance. Surely no one can side step this book (it is really a library of books). It is attacked by some, ignored by many others and misunderstood by multitudes. But it still remains the world's best seller, translated into more world languages than any other set of writings.

Why not start with John's Gospel. It was written by an old man who had perhaps been only a teenager when Jesus came into his life. He was an eye witness to the conversations that he invites you to listen in to. They had meant so much to him and Jesus had made such an enormous difference to his life that he refused to die before he got it all down in writing. Pick up his book. Listen in and see what happens.

Prayer:
Lord, we are grateful that you have not left us without direction for all of life and that, simply by taking up your word and reading it, we can listen in on your thoughts. Amen.

Battle for the mind

*Therefore, I urge you, brothers, in view of God's
mercy, to offer your bodies as living sacrifices, holy
and pleasing to God – this is your spiritual act of
worship. Do not conform any longer to the pattern
of this world, but be transformed by the renewing of
your mind. Then you will be able to test and approve
what God's will is – his good, pleasing and perfect
will. For by the grace given me I say to every one of
you: Do not think of yourself more highly than you
ought, but rather think of yourself with sober
judgment, in accordance with the measure of faith
God has given you.*

(Romans 12:1–3)

•••

'Drive me!' says the new model car. 'Smoke me!'
says the latest brand of cigarette. 'Drink me!' says
the new bottle of something. 'Vote for me!' says the
campaigning politician. And the poor citizen, over
whose mind and allegiance the whole world seems
to be fighting, cries 'Pity me!'.

Everyone with something to sell knows how
important the mind is. And so does God. He knows
that our thinking can be what he calls 'futile' and
badly in need of renewal. He wants us to use our
minds in a way that harmonises with his.

I once saw a couple of cartoons. The first was of a
king and queen, gazing through the palace window

at rioting peasants. The king says 'If only I could force them to love me'. In the second cartoon an angry picketer carries a placard which says 'If you're for it I'm against it'. The king had no way of controlling the minds of his subjects, the picketer's mind-set was so contrary that he would spoil for a fight no matter what the issue was.

Who is in charge of your mind? What do you allow into it? That super-computer between your ears is a very powerful instrument; it determines your outward actions by its inward programming. Programme it with sex, violence, pride, prejudice or whatever and you will soon be immoral, violent, arrogant and bigoted.

God offers us a process of divine re-programming. We can, with Christ's help, be 'renewed in the spirit of our minds'. Initially this occurs in a wonderful new birth and then, with the mind under new management, we start to feed it with a new and health-giving diet. With ingredients such as Bible reading, prayer and Christian fellowship, our inner life begins to surface as a truly Christian life-style.

Prayer:
O God, Creator of body, mind and spirit, take my thought processes under your control. Help me to turn away from those influences that corrupt and destroy, and help me to open up to the healthy, life-giving influence of your Spirit. For Jesus' sake. Amen.

'The might have beens'

So, as the Holy Spirit says: 'Today, if you hear his voice, do not harden your hearts as you did in the rebellion, during the time of testing in the desert, where your fathers tested and tried me and for forty years saw what I did. That is why I was angry with that generation, and I said, "Their hearts are always going astray, and they have not known my ways." So I declared on oath in my anger, "They shall never enter my rest".'

See to it, brothers, that none of you has a sinful, unbelieving heart that turns away from the living God. But encourage one another daily, as long as it is called Today, so that none of you may be hardened by sin's deceitfulness. We have come to share in Christ if we hold firmly till the end the confidence we had at first. As has just been said: 'Today, if you hear his voice, do not harden your hearts as you did in the rebellion.'

(Hebrews 3:7–15)

●●●

Charles Lamb wrote of a man called Samuel Le Grice, a brilliant youth who never fulfilled his potential. Lamb noted three stages in this man's career: the time when people said 'he will do something'; the time when they said 'he could do something'; and the time when they said 'he might have done something'. His life was one big 'might have been'.

William Barclay wrote of Samuel Taylor Coleridge, 'never did a great mind produce so little'. He left Cambridge University to join the army. He left the army because he could not groom a horse. He returned to university (Oxford this time) but left without a degree. He began a newspaper but it only ran to ten issues. He envisaged work that needed to be done (he had many unwritten books in his head) but he never got round to producing them.

I suspect that most of us grieve a bit over powers which have never been realised, qualities that have never been developed, resolutions never acted upon. What a challenge to do a bit of stock-taking! What will be said of us as we reach the end of life? Will our epitaph be 'glad I did' or will it be 'I wish I had'.

The Bible says you reap what you sow. So how we invest our lives now has eternal consequences, resulting in things that will forever make us sad or glad. It has been said that there are four things that never return:

the spoken word
the sped arrow
the past life
the neglected opportunity.

Prayer:
O God, time is flying and there is so much in us that has never been put to its rightful use. Forgive us for our slothful ways and dangerous lack of discipline. Give us the resolve to take hold of life and make the very best of what we have in the days to come. Amen.

Sheep, goats – or humans?

Rejoice in the Lord always. I will say it again: Rejoice!
Let your gentleness be evident to all. The Lord is
near. Do not be anxious about anything, but in
everything, by prayer and petition, with thanksgiving,
present your requests to God. And the peace of God,
which transcends all understanding, will guard your
hearts and your minds in Christ Jesus.

Finally, brothers, whatever is true, whatever is noble,
whatever is right, whatever is pure, whatever is
lovely, whatever is admirable – if anything is
excellent or praiseworthy – think about such things.

(Philippians 4:4–8)

●●●

'More things are wrought by prayer than this
world dreams of: For what are men better than
sheep or goats, if, knowing God, they lift not hands
of prayer both for themselves and those who call
them friend.'

So said Tennyson, and we all agree – at least in
principle. But when it comes to practice we are
mostly very slow to pray. It should be our first step
but is often our last. It is our highest privilege but
often our lowest priority. We talk to Tom, Dick and
Harry, and Betty too, before we talk to God.

Why should we pass up the opportunity to talk to
our greatest confidant and friend? Why should we
shoulder heavy loads that he is willing to carry?

One answer to these hard questions probably arises from misconceptions about prayer. People often think of it as a mysterious activity best practised in a church building or at the bed side. It requires folded hands and tough knees and the ability to use 17th century English containing many 'thees' and 'thous'. Another misconception is that if God is as powerful as he is said to be why can't he do things without hearing from us?

Prayer is really just talking to God. Conversation. Telling him our problems. Asking for help. Expressing our appreciation of him. Seeking his advice. Listening. Waiting. Meditating. Praying is giving our families and friends into God's hands.

There is no need of a special time or place. It can be done standing, sitting, walking, in the bath or on the bed. It can be done in the car (but keep your eyes open if you are driving!) God is there. God is listening. Pray!

Prayer:
'Lord, teach us to pray'.

17

How does God guide?

Yet the LORD longs to be gracious to you; he rises to show you compassion. For the LORD is a God of justice. Blessed are all who wait for him!
O people of Zion, who live in Jerusalem, you will weep no more. How gracious he will be when you cry for help! As soon as he hears, he will answer you. Although the Lord gives you the bread of adversity and the water of affliction, your teachers will be hidden no more; with your own eyes you will see them. Whether you turn to the right or to the left, your ears will hear a voice behind you, saying, 'This is the way; walk in it.'

(Isaiah 30:18–21)

●●●

I used to think that the guidance of God was a mysterious, difficult and complex matter. However, as I looked more deeply into it, I found it began to simplify. I took note of the many promises in the Bible that assured me that guidance was available. I also noted that these promises seem to depend on me having a surrendered will, a seeking heart and a teachable mind. So now, if I am seeking guidance, I believe that God will give it to me, I actively seek for it and I surrender my will to accept it.

Some of the key means of guidance are:

• *The word of Scripture:* The Bible has many commands and prohibitions and about those there can be no argument – you do not need guidance about whether you should be loving or whether you should steal things! But, in addition, there are times when a particular passage or verse from the Bible comes alive to you in a special way.

- *Conscience:* God often uses this inner censor to keep us on track.
- *A sense of the rightness of something:* We get God's peace on the matter in question and this gives us an inner calm about doing or not doing it.
- *God's still, small voice:* This is not an audible voice but an undeniable sense of being prompted by God. It is often a quiet but persistent hunch about which people often say 'I just could not get it out of my mind'.
- *Circumstances:* Doors of opportunity can open, sometimes quite suddenly. And just as clearly other openings can be closed off to us. This can sometimes be the simplest form of guidance – even if we don't like it all that much!
- *A word of advice:* Family and friends, colleagues, fellow church members and other Christians can often help us choose the right path. Being people who love us and want the best for us and being also people of prayer who seek God's will, they can sometimes see aspects that we have missed.
- *Our own preferences and common sense:* God has given all of us minds to think with and if we are surrendered to him, then thinking about the right course of action is not an unspiritual thing to do.

Prayer:
Lord, give me a believing heart, a surrendered will and a sensible mind so that I may know your will and do it. Amen.

In a rut

This is what the LORD says – your Redeemer, the
Holy One of Israel: 'For your sake I will send to
Babylon and bring down as fugitives all the
Babylonians, in the ships in which they took pride. I
am the LORD, your Holy One, Israel's Creator, your
King.'
This is what the LORD says – he who made a way
through the sea, a path through the mighty waters,
who drew out the chariots and horses, the army and
reinforcements together, and they lay there, never to
rise again, extinguished, snuffed out like a wick:
'Forget the former things; do not dwell on the past.
See, I am doing a new thing! Now it springs up; do
you not perceive it? I am making a way in the
desert and streams in the wasteland. The wild
animals honour me, the jackals and the owls,
because I provide water in the desert and streams
in the wasteland, to give drink to my people, my
chosen, the people I formed for myself that they
may proclaim my praise.'

(Isaiah 43:14–21)

●●●

I suppose sometimes we all feel that we are in a
bit of a rut. But if we resign ourselves to our rut we
become stuck in a rut. The sad thing is that a rut is
really a hangover from a path which once actually
led somewhere. It is just that it has been walked over

so often that its original creativity has been lost: a rut is an overgrown path.

We start off, excited by the direction we take. But, perhaps because of dull conservatism or laziness or carelessness we get shackled to yesterday's patterns. Life moves on but we are left behind, stuck in our rut. Sometimes it is past successes that make it so hard for us to leave our entrenched ways. The 'good old days' were great but new days have come.

We have to ask the hard and painful questions: 'is this thing still worth doing?' and 'is it worth doing this way?' 'Am I in a rut, a groove that has turned into a grave?'

Peter Drucker in his book *The Effective Executive* says 'there is no lack of ideas in any organisation I know. But few organisations ever get going on their good ideas. Everybody is much too busy with the tasks of yesterday'.

What would happen if every church regularly put its programmes and procedures on trial? What new vistas might open up? What creative ideas might come to light? How liberating it might be. And what about us as individuals? Perhaps we need to change, to leave the rut and strike out in new directions. God says 'if anyone is in Christ, he is a new creation: the old has gone, the new has come'.

It is not too late to bring our programmes, our habits, our life-style, our families, ourselves to the Christ who still says 'behold I make all things new'.

Prayer:
Lord, help me to be more honest with myself as I look over what I am and what I do. Help me to bring it all to you to check and evaluate and then give me the courage to change if that is necessary. For Jesus' sake. Amen.

Dad – What is God like?

These are the commands, decrees and laws the LORD your God directed me to teach you to observe in the land that you are crossing the Jordan to possess, so that you, your children and their children after them may fear the LORD your God as long as you live by keeping all his decrees and commands that I give you, and so that you may enjoy long life. Hear, O Israel, and be careful to obey so that it may go well with you and that you may increase greatly in a land flowing with milk and honey, just as the LORD, the God of your fathers, promised you.

Hear, O Israel: The LORD our God, the LORD is one. Love the LORD your God with all your heart and with all your soul and with all your strength. These commandments that I give you today are to be upon your hearts. Impress them on your children. Talk about them when you sit at home and when you walk along the road, when you lie down and when you get up. Tie them as symbols on your hands and bind them on your foreheads. Write them on the doorframes of your houses and on your gates.

(Deuteronomy 6:1–9)

● ● ●

Our team was conducting a mission at the University of the Witwatersrand in South Africa.

One of the professors said to us 'I'm backing this mission, because my children are asking me the $1,000 question, and I need an answer myself'. I imagine that many parents could identify with the Professor's confession. Children have an uncanny ability to ask major questions about human destiny. And they want answers because parental bluffing won't wash. At least not for long.

A child asked her mother 'where did I come from' and was told that she was brought by the stork. She got the same answer when she asked about the coming of her mother and her grandfather. 'Heavens', she said, 'there hasn't been a natural birth in this family for three generations'.

We hope that today's parents are better than that at explaining the facts of life. But what about the big spiritual issues? How is it when parents have no answers? Some parents profess to take the high moral ground by saying 'we don't want to influence our children one way or the other. They must decide for themselves when they are older'. Is this adult conviction or adult confusion?

The Bible certainly does not encourage parents to be neutral about their children's spiritual growth. It urges us to 'train' them to follow God's directions for life. This means we ourselves need to know the way and have strong convictions about it. It also suggests a gradual and continual process lasting through childhood into young adulthood. And some things are 'caught' from us as well as taught by us and that includes our failure to have convictions or give a spiritual lead.

Jesus felt so strongly about this that he said it was better to be dropped into the sea with a millstone round your neck than to cause one of these little ones to stumble. So the Professor was on the right track for himself and for his children.

Prayer:

Dear Father in heaven, we look to you, our Perfect Parent, to assist us in being good and godly guides to those special young lives that you have put into our hands. Please help us not to fail in showing them who you are and how they should live. Amen.

The ultimate epitaph

And do not grieve the Holy Spirit of God, with whom you were sealed for the day of redemption. Get rid of all bitterness, rage and anger, brawling and slander, along with every form of malice. Be kind and compassionate to one another, forgiving each other, just as in Christ God forgave you. Be imitators of God, therefore, as dearly loved children and live a life of love, just as Christ loved us and gave himself up for us as a fragrant offering and sacrifice to God.

(Ephesians 4:30–5:2)

●●●

In a cemetery near New York is a gravestone, stark and strikingly simple. It has no name on it, no date of birth or date of death. It has only one inscription: 'forgiven'.

This may seem odd. Were there no other significant things about the person buried there? Perhaps there were, but, when you think about it, for a human being to know the forgiveness of God is the ultimate blessing of life. It means that the barrier between God and that person has gone. It means that he or she has accepted Christ's sacrifice for sins and been accepted eternally by God. It means that the ultimate price has been paid and that it has also been accepted by God and by the forgiven sinner.

Some people baulk at the idea of Christ having to

pay the price for us. Why could God not have simply forgiven us without all that suffering and sacrifice? Well, think about it this way. If someone stole $10 from me and I forgave him, it still costs me $10. Indeed the greater the sum, the greater the cost of forgiveness. If someone slanders me I forgive him at the cost of my reputation. If someone stabs me I forgive him at the cost of my wounds.

Christianity declares that humanity has committed the ultimate offence. We – through our representatives at the time – killed the Son of God in the name of religion and political expediency. This was the ultimate crime and it involved the ultimate cost and won for us the ultimate forgiveness. When we accept this for ourselves, the word 'forgiven' becomes the most significant thing that could ever be said about us.

Jesus forgave from the cross. Not from an armchair up in heaven or on a grassy bank by the sea. From the cross. And those who are forgiven are then duty bound to forgive others. Vertical forgiveness from God and horizontal forgiveness to others are unalterably wedded. Perhaps a better epitaph would be 'forgiven and forgiving'.

Prayer:
Dear Lord, we are staggered at the cost by which we are forgiven. Help us never to undervalue what Jesus has done for us or to forget our responsibility to pass on forgiveness to other people. For Jesus' sake. Amen.

Holy Joe and Sinful Sam

(Jesus) told his next story to some who were complacently pleased with themselves over their moral performance and looked down their noses at the common people: "Two men went up to the Temple to pray, one a Pharisee, the other a tax man. The Pharisee posed and prayed like this: 'O God , I thank you that I am not like other people —robbers, crooks, adulterers, or, heaven forbid, like this tax man. I fast twice a week and tithe on all my income'.

"Meanwhile the tax man, slumped in the shadows, his face in his hands, not daring to look up, said, 'God give mercy. Forgive me, a sinner.'"

Jesus commented, "This tax man, not the other, went home made right with God. If you walk around with your nose in the air, you're going to end up flat on your face, but if you're content to be simply yourself, you will become more than yourself."

(Luke 18:9–14 from The Message by Eugene Peterson)

●●●

Two men went into the church to pray. One of them, Holy Joe, was extremely religious. The other, was a rather petty public servant for whom things had gone terribly wrong. His name was Sinful Sam and the two men could hardly have been more different from each other.

Joe was a passionate churchgoer. He subscribed to church magazines and often wrote to the editor about great matters such as the choir boys' robes and the church heating system. He was on many church committees and enjoyed power under the cloak of altruism. He was a generous giver but he did like his gifts to be noticed by others. He read the Bible, said his prayers and could argue nice theological points with accuracy and passion. Morally, he kept the rules and he could be pretty scathing about those who flouted them.

Being such a paragon of virtue it was small wonder that he was shocked to see Sinful Sam at the back of the church. Sam was notorious, one of the town's more questionable characters (Holy Joe could not imagine how he could tie down a job with the Taxation Department). Some rumours had it that he had a drink problem and had recently flattened one of his drinking mates in one of the local pubs. What was he doing in church!

Holy Joe's prayer was a catalogue of his virtues. He told God how grateful he was that he was not like Sam. But Sam's prayer was a short staccato cry for mercy: 'God have mercy on me, sinner that I am'. Joe's prayer hit the ceiling and rebounded. Sam's prayer went right through the roof into the very presence of God. Jesus said he was the one who went home acquitted.

Prayer:
Lord, I cannot bring my virtues to you because they are very weak and poor things and tainted with selfishness. But I can and I do bring my sins to you and plead for your mercy and forgiveness, all because of Jesus and his sacrifice on the cross. Amen.

22

Are Christians escapists?

By faith we understand that the universe was formed at God's command, so that what is seen was not made out of what was visible. By faith Abel offered God a better sacrifice than Cain did. By faith he was commended as a righteous man, when God spoke well of his offerings. And by faith he still speaks, even though he is dead. By faith Enoch was taken from this life, so that he did not experience death; he could not be found, because God had taken him away. For before he was taken, he was commended as one who pleased God. And without faith it is impossible to please God, because anyone who comes to him must believe that he exists and that he rewards those who earnestly seek him.

(Hebrews 11:3–6)

●●●

One of the misrepresentations of Christians is that they are fleeing from reality and are weaklings who need a religious 'crutch' to help them face life.

I object! I submit that when Christians are true to themselves and their Lord they are supremely realistic and can look all the data of life in the face unafraid. For example, they do not try to escape from God. They know him to be the great Cause which explains the Effect and therefore the very source and centre of reality.

Neither do Christians escape from science. They

believe that scientific thought actually depends on some presuppositions that are basically theological, that is, the regularity, predictability and uniformity of things. As C.S. Lewis wrote 'Our repugnance to disorder is derived from nature's Creator and ours. The disorderly world which we cannot endure to believe in is the disorderly world God would not have endured to create'.

Thirdly, Christians do not escape from what has been called 'the moral environment'. The philosopher Immanuel Kant said that he was impressed by two things, 'the starry sky above and the moral law within'. But many people today deny the source of such a law. They judge some things to be either good or evil, they disapprove of actions such as theft, cruelty and injustice, they are convinced that it is better to be a St Francis than an Adolf Hitler. They imagine that such standards are self explanatory without realising that they originate in a God who is infinitely good.

Above all, Christians have no need to escape from themselves. They face the facts about themselves and then accept and forgive themselves because what they are has been accepted and forgiven by God. The central fact of their faith is that God himself, through Jesus Christ, has personally dealt with their guilt and failure and re-established his own moral standards within them. They have nothing to fear in life – or in death.

Prayer:
O Great God of order, truth and harmony we rejoice in the reality of our faith. Keep us true to ourselves, upright in our actions and honest to God. Amen.

23

The unhappy hippy

The Samaritan woman said to him, 'You are a Jew and I am a Samaritan woman. How can you ask me for a drink?' (For Jews do not associate with Samaritans.) Jesus answered her, 'If you knew the gift of God and who it is that asks you for a drink, you would have asked him and he would have given you living water.' 'Sir,' the woman said, 'you have nothing to draw with and the well is deep. Where can you get this living water? Are you greater than our father Jacob, who gave us the well and drank from it himself, as did also his sons and his flocks and herds?' Jesus answered, 'Everyone who drinks this water will be thirsty again, but whoever drinks the water I give him will never thirst. Indeed, the water I give him will become in him a spring of water welling up to eternal life.'

(John 4:9–14)

●●●

He gazed at me with intense but slightly bloodshot eyes. 'Do I look like a hippy?' he asked, fumbling for a cigarette. 'No, I don't think so, I, er…' 'Well, I am. I am what they call a Hillbrow Hippy. I go with the gang here. I take drugs, smoke pot, drink and all the rest. But I am as unhappy as hell'.

He pulled his chair close. 'It might surprise you to know that I come from a good home and went to a good school. I used to go to church. But somehow I got away from it all. I've become more and more miserable. Everything's so lost and hopeless. It got me down and I decided to come to this church tonight. The sermon kind of got to me – about Jesus being able to help and all that. So I stayed on when he invited us to stay and talk. I thought: Why not? Could Jesus do anything for someone like me?'

'He certainly can do something for you', I said. 'He can change your life and give you peace and purpose – a new start.' 'Really?' he said, 'you mean someone as bad as me?'

'Yes' I said, 'that's what the Gospel is all about. Changing people. Any people. If they really want it.'

He lit another cigarette, 'Keep talking'.

I told him of Jesus' love for people, especially lost people, about his offer of forgiveness and his gift of the Holy Spirit to change lives. And about fifteen minutes later he bowed his head and invited Jesus Christ into his life. Months later the minister at that church told me, 'he's a transformed person and a happy member of this church'.

The Gospel is for unhappy hippies or whoever you like to name. As St Paul said 'if a man is in Christ, he becomes a new person – the past is finished and gone, everything has become fresh and new'.

Prayer:
Lord what a wonderful gift to us is your life-changing gospel. What a change it works in those who sincerely accept it and the marvellous forgiveness which it promises. Please help us to value it for ourselves, and for others. For Jesus' sake. Amen.

24

Dr Livingstone I presume

Therefore, since we are surrounded by such a great cloud of witnesses, let us throw off everything that hinders and the sin that so easily entangles, and let us run with perseverance the race marked out for us. Let us fix our eyes on Jesus, the author and perfecter of our faith, who for the joy set before him endured the cross, scorning its shame, and sat down at the right hand of the throne of God. Consider him who endured such opposition from sinful men, so that you will not grow weary and lose heart. In your struggle against sin, you have not yet resisted to the point of shedding your blood. And you have forgotten that word of encouragement that addresses you as sons: 'My son, do not make light of the Lord's discipline, and do not lose heart when he rebukes you.'

(Hebrews 12:1–5)

•••

In 1870 Henry Morton Stanley got one of the greatest assignments in the history of journalism. He was commissioned to find the famous Dr Livingstone. 'I think he is alive', said the Editor of *The New York Herald*, 'and he can be found'. So it was, in many ways, a venture of faith.

If you read Stanley's journal you will live with him through the agonies and the ecstasies of his quest. You cannot but marvel at the lengths to which he went and at the way he met and overcame his trials and tribulations. His eventual discovery of the great man gave him the biggest thrill and the greatest anticlimax of his life. He wrote:

> What would I not have given for a bit of friendly wilderness, where unseen I might vent my joy in some mad frolic, such as idiotically biting my hand, turning somersaults or slashing at trees in order to allay those exciting feelings that were well nigh uncontrollable. My heart beats fast, but I must not let my face betray my emotions, lest it shall detract from the dignity of a white man appearing under such extraordinary circumstances. I would have run to him, only I was a coward in the presence of such a mob – would have embraced him, only, he being an Englishman, I did not know how he would receive me: so I did what cowardice and false pride suggested was the best thing – walked to him, took off my hat and said: 'Dr Livingstone, I presume?' 'Yes', he said with a kind smile, lifting his cap slightly.

For Stanley the great moment was over and there was soon a great emptiness. The quest was over. The great missionary was found. In the end Stanley died a famous but bitter and disappointed man.

In Christ there is no such anticlimax. The trials of faith and the agonies of the journey are all worthwhile and the end of the quest will be still fulfilling. And, we presume, Livingstone would entirely agree.

Prayer:
Lord Jesus, we are so glad that finding you is no disappointment. We travel on towards heaven full of conviction that what we have found here will be even better when we get to our journey's end. Amen.

25

Unmuzzle the lion

In the temple courts he found men selling cattle, sheep and doves, and others sitting at tables exchanging money. So he made a whip out of cords, and drove all from the temple area, both sheep and cattle; he scattered the coins of the money changers and overturned their tables. To those who sold doves he said, 'Get these out of here! How dare you turn my Father's house into a market!' His disciples remembered that it is written: 'Zeal for your house will consume me.'

(John 2:14–17)

●●●

I have an objection. We have tamed Jesus. We have fossilised him in antiquity, watered him down and made him docile. We have cluttered him up with cliches and jargon. We have muzzled the Lion.

Not only that, but we have trimmed his claws and tried to sell him to the world as a harmless pussy cat. To Sunday school kids we have presented him with pink cheeks and curls and taken the muscles from his arms, the fire from his eyes and the uncompromising demands from his lips. To round off we have made him boring, turned a revolutionary into a relic and muffled the most radical personality of human history.

To some of his contemporaries Jesus was far from boring, he was a dangerous fire-brand. They got out of his way as he stormed through the temple, overturning tables and hunting the money changers out the door. At the end of his life, single-handed he took on the city crowds, the religious powers-that-be and even the imperial Roman government. And he did all this long before modern democracy had made radicalism safe.

Who was he? This carpenter revolutionary who lived in poverty and obscurity. He never travelled or wrote a book or marshalled an army and he was finally executed as a common criminal. But every week in nearly every nation under heaven, great multitudes of people gather together to worship him and respond to what he taught.

Who was he? Let us hear his own assessment of himself: 'I am the way, and the truth, and the life. No one comes to the father except through me. If you really knew me, you would know my Father as well … he who has seen me has seen the father'.

So off with the muzzle and away with the jargon and the feeble caricatures. Let the Lion speak for himself.

Prayer:
O Lord Jesus, Lion of Judah and King of Kings, we have sometimes misrepresented you in the weak and wobbly way in which we have presented you to the world. Please give us the grace and courage to tell the real truth about you. Amen.

26

Space for God

Now faith is being sure of what we hope for and certain of what we do not see. This is what the ancients were commended for. By faith we understand that the universe was formed at God's command, so that what is seen was not made out of what was visible.

(Hebrews 11:1–3)

●●●

In 1997 millions of people used an Internet website for a glimpse of *Sojourner,* the busy little NASA robot, sniffing at rocks on the planet Mars. Back in 1969, 600 million television watchers saw the moon landing and Neil Armstrong taking his 'giant step for mankind'.

With such spectacular successes it is easy to forget earlier space adventures. One of these was Apollo 8 and the first manned orbit of the moon. As the astronauts gazed on its bare inhospitable surface and then looked back at the beautiful blue planet from which they had come, they were moved to read from the book of Genesis: 'in the beginning God created the heavens and the earth…' In the midst of humanity's greatest scientific achievement they were filled with wonder at what God had done.

Of course this was an act of faith. It was a conviction that the universe was created and did not simply happen. But it was a conviction which science could neither prove nor disprove, since it concentrates on the 'seen' world, whereas theology focuses on the 'unseen' or spiritual world. Science works on 'what?' and 'how?', theology on 'who?' and 'why?'. Science observes data and experiments with it, faith looks to its source and origin. Far from being vague and insubstantial, faith believes that 'what is seen is temporary, but what is unseen is eternal'.

The Genesis from which the astronauts read is not, of course, a scientific document. Its account is couched in beautiful ageless words, describing creation from the viewpoint of a human observer. It is a powerful testimony to the essential truth that God put all things together in an orderly fashion with man, made in his image, the crown of his handiwork. And God the Father was author and initiator of creation; God the Son was agent. 'For by him all things were created: things in heaven and on earth, visible and invisible ... all things were created by him and for him.'

So when the orbiting astronauts looked at the moon and the earth and acknowledged them to be the work of God, this was testimony to the further belief that we acknowledge Christ as God. For the Christian faith makes that claim: that the lovely planet on which we live has been visited by God in the person of Jesus Christ. And unless we come to terms with this, all our glittering scientific achievements will be fruitless. We may master the moon and maybe also Mars; we may scientifically conquer other worlds. But if, in arrogant intellectual triumph, we stand among the debris of moral and spiritual decadence, it will all be futile.

Prayer:

O Lord Jesus, Lord of the universe, we thank you for the wonder of scientific achievement and we pray that we will ascribe each wonderful discovery to our great Saviour. Amen

27

The Thomas syndrome

*Now Thomas (called Didymus), one of the Twelve,
was not with the disciples when Jesus came. So the
other disciples told him, 'We have seen the Lord!' But
he said to them, 'Unless I see the nail marks in his
hands and put my finger where the nails were, and
put my hand into his side, I will not believe it.' A
week later his disciples were in the house again, and
Thomas was with them. Though the doors were
locked, Jesus came and stood among them and said,
'Peace be with you!' Then he said to Thomas, 'Put
your finger here; see my hands. Reach out your hand
and put it into my side. Stop doubting and believe.'
Thomas said to him, 'My Lord and my God!' Then
Jesus told him, 'Because you have seen me, you have
believed; blessed are those who have not seen and
yet have believed.' Jesus did many other miraculous
signs in the presence of his disciples, which are not
recorded in this book. But these are written that you
may believe that Jesus is the Christ, the Son of God,
and that by believing you may have life in his name.*
(John 20:24–31)

●●●

Doubting Thomas is one of the Bible's most
attractive characters. He was an honest doubter who
asked hard questions but was glad of good answers.
Such doubt is certainly preferable to hypocrisy. And
also preferable to the 'doubt' behind which some

people hide their spiritual nakedness and moral rebellion. Their problem is not intellectual but moral. It is dodging, not doubting.

Jesus knew that Thomas was no phoney. He seemed to understand and sympathise with him. Jesus' promise to people like him was: ask and it will be given to you; seek and you will find; knock and the door will be opened to you.

Doubt has many causes. An obvious one is simply a lack of intellectual conviction about what seems incredible. That was Thomas' problem and since Christian commitment never involves intellectual suicide, Jesus eventually gave Thomas the evidence he sought. Some doubters who were convinced by the evidence have written helpfully about it. Try Frank Morison's *Who Moved The Stone?* or *Mere Christianity* by C.S. Lewis.

Sometimes doubt is precipitated by unfortunate experiences. Someone has had religion rammed down their throat at home or at school. Or he or she has inherited family scepticism or been hurt or disappointed by a regular churchgoer. But the truth of Christianity does not depend on the strengths or weaknesses of Christians but on the reality of Jesus and his resurrection from the dead. Focus on that.

The problem of suffering and evil can be the cause for some doubt: how can a good God allow bad things? In one sense, whether you believe or not, there is no solution to this riddle except in coming to the cross of Christ and seeing how mankind's greatest crime was transformed into God's greatest redemption for humankind. And Christians have learned that this victory keeps working for them, continually putting silver linings on the darkest clouds.

Thomas asked his doubting questions and eventually got substantial answers. He saw in Jesus and his wounded hands and side the ultimate answer to all life's riddles. He knelt before him and acclaimed him 'my Lord and my God'. And Jesus, glad that Thomas had now believed because he had visible proof, said that there was an even better response: 'blessed are those who have not seen and yet have believed'. And that is where you and I come in.

Prayer:
Lord, in an age of doubt and scepticism, help us to stay focused on the Lord Jesus, crucified, risen and victorious over sin and death. Lord, we believe that if he is not the answer then there is no answer! Amen.

28

Spiritual Olympics

*Do you not know that in a race all the runners run,
but only one gets the prize? Run in such a way as to
get the prize. Everyone who competes in the games
goes into strict training. They do it to get a crown
that will not last; but we do it to get a crown that
will last forever. Therefore I do not run like a man
running aimlessly; I do not fight like a man beating
the air. No, I beat my body and make it my slave so
that after I have preached to others, I myself will
not be disqualified for the prize.*

(1 Corinthians 9:24–27)

●●●

Aussies are going to find it hard to avoid Olympic
fever. Television and radio will be increasingly full of
it, pictures of the progress at Homebush Bay will be
seen daily in the newspapers and athletes and their
chances at winning will be discussed by the pundits.

How strange that competitions that started in the
9th or 10th century BC and which were celebrated
every five years in honour of the god Zeus should
occupy the minds and energies of people today! In
those far off days, to be crowned as Olympic victor
with the garland of olive twigs was the ultimate
honour. Songs were sung in the victor's praise;
statues raised in his honour and he would have free
board and lodging whenever he came to Athens.

The sports-loving Greeks attached so much

importance to the games that they reckoned time by the four year periods between the Games. But in the 194th Olympiad someone was born who lived to change all that. Jesus Christ became the new hinge of history so that in due course the old chronologies were reworked around the letters BC and AD. But he changed more than the system of dating; after him human values, human honours, even the Olympic garland, became trivial beside the Ultimate Prize of finding him.

Paul the Apostle, great communicator that he was, soon saw the athletic contests as the ideal illustration of running the Christian race. Not looking backwards, we strain towards the great prize that awaits us: 'the prize for which God has called me heavenward in Christ Jesus'. I suppose that it never ceased to surprise Paul, who was probably no four-minute miler, that people could go though such incredible physical exertion to gain such transitory honours while they ignored the bigger issue of winning or losing eternally. What was the value of human acclaim and the wreath of rapidly withering leaves if, at the end of life, you lost the biggest race of all?

Paul remembers the strict training schedule of the athletes, the way they put their all into the race and he says to his Corinthian friends, 'run with your minds fixed on the prize, don't lose your concentration or be side-tracked from the course in front of you. Run! Run for your life!'

Prayer:
Dear heavenly Father, keep us on track and running well in the Christian race. Help us to run hard and to keep on running right to the end. For Jesus' sake. Amen.

29

Forgiving and forgetting

Get rid of all bitterness, rage and anger, brawling and slander, along with every form of malice. Be kind and compassionate to one another, forgiving each other, just as in Christ God forgave you. Be imitators of God, therefore, as dearly loved children and live a life of love, just as Christ loved us and gave himself up for us as a fragrant offering and sacrifice to God.

(Ephesians 4:31–5:2)

●●●

Cultivating a good memory is important. But equally useful is developing a good 'forgettery'. Whereas the first is natural and simply needs cultivating, the second goes against the grain and often involves a struggle.

There are things which are difficult to forget. Sometimes words and actions from the past live on to jeopardise the present and the future. Such things can spread like a malignant cancer till they weaken the whole of life. Those who do not understand and accept the forgiveness of God are unable to free themselves and forget the crippling past.

The Bible is full of promises of forgiveness for those who confess their sins to God; God says 'I will forgive their wickedness and remember their sins no more'. The prophet Micah said of God that he would 'hurl all our iniquities into the depths of the sea' and Corrie ten Boom remarked that when God said that, he put up a sign No Fishing!

This kind of forgetting relates to what we ourselves have done in relation to God and other people. But there is another kind that I suspect is even harder than the first one: it is learning to forget what others have said and done to us. Things said can never be unsaid, things done can never be undone. And life being what it is and people being what they are, we will often be confronted with the need to forgive and with our incapacity to do so. We seethe and writhe with resentment and sometimes we even horrify ourselves with thoughts of retaliation and reprisal.

I am sure that the first step in recovering our spiritual equilibrium is to recognise our own sinfulness and need of Christ's forgiveness. And then to realise the need to forgive others. This gives us a new motivation in dealing with and overcoming our own unwillingness to forgive. When we have gotten that far, the next step is surely to pray for the offending party because hatred and prayer cannot co-exist for long. Praying for people opens our eyes to their needs and problems and perhaps to what caused them to give us pain. Compassion replaces resentment and we are ready to talk with them and start again.

We forgive – and we forget.

Prayer:
Dear Lord, how we need to be forgiven! And how we need to be forgiven for our own unforgiveness! Cleanse us and renew us, fill us with your love and mercy and teach us how to forgive and forget. For Jesus' sake. Amen.

30

The X factor

In the beginning was the Word, and the Word was with God, and the Word was God. He was with God in the beginning. Through him all things were made; without him nothing was made that has been made. In him was life, and that life was the light of men. The light shines in the darkness, but the darkness has not understood it. There came a man who was sent from God; his name was John. He came as a witness to testify concerning that light, so that through him all men might believe. He himself was not the light; he came only as a witness to the light. The true light that gives light to every man was coming into the world.

(John 1:1–9).

●●●

Christians have often suspected that calling Christmas 'Xmas' was a secular attempt to manoeuvre Christ out of a mention on his own birthday. If you take the religion out of the festival you can make it as commercial or as materialistic as you like. Or else you can turn it into a 'family festival' especially for the kids. Whichever way you do it, Christ has become 'X', as remote as an algebraic sign.

Although I barely scraped through my maths finals, I do remember that 'X' generally stood for the baffling part of an equation which it was your job to figure out. It was the unknown quantity which you had to struggle to decipher. And I suppose for many people Christ is a bit like that, a mysterious unknown figure who refuses to be removed from life's equation. He is the supreme X factor.

Whoever he was, X certainly started something. In three short years he lit a fire that 20 centuries of human history have not been able to extinguish. He did it without ever appearing on coast-to-coast TV, without writing a single book, without catapulting round the world in a jet plane. Nor did he appear to have the right training for such a big undertaking; born into a peasant family and working as a village tradesman, his *curriculum vitae* would have contained no degrees from the best schools and universities.

But X was good, devastatingly good. There was no room in him for hatred or lust or revenge or cruelty and his peerless character has a way of showing us up so starkly that we are either driven to despair or trapped by its magnetism. The trouble is that the dark side of our nature is so delicious and addictive. As X said of us, we love the darkness and are more at home with it than we are with the light. He saw our poor old planet as dominated by darkness and he saw himself as its true Light, its only hope.

Sometimes at Xmas there does seem to be a bit more light around, some love, kindness and goodwill. People laugh a bit more and the kids are full of excitement and anticipation. It almost seems as though a bit of X is coming through and we wish it would last. But often the armistice only lasts for about 24 hours and then we are back to business, back to darkness, to anger, lust and revenge.

You know it is crazy that we do not stick to X when once a year we get a tiny glimpse of how he can change things and how his mercy can wash away the past and give us a new start. Those who open up to him permanently find that the Light comes to stay and that it challenges and opposes the darkness inside of us. It is then that X ceases to be the unknown factor and becomes the solution to the whole equation.

Prayer:
Lord Jesus, Light of the world, come in today, come in to stay and make our lives Christmas every day. Amen.

31

The stony path to becoming a rock

When Jesus came to the region of Caesarea Philippi, he asked his disciples, 'Who do people say the Son of Man is?' They replied, 'Some say John the Baptist; others say Elijah; and still others, Jeremiah or one of the prophets.' 'But what about you?' he asked. 'Who do you say I am?' Simon Peter answered, 'You are the Christ, the Son of the living God.' Jesus replied, 'Blessed are you, Simon son of Jonah, for this was not revealed to you by man, but by my Father in heaven. And I tell you that you are Peter, and on this rock I will build my church, and the gates of Hades will not overcome it.'

(Matthew 16:13–18)

●●●

Most people find it hard to believe that they could change. They feel that they are saddled forever with a lot of things they don't much like such as temper, doubt, instability. They think they can do nothing; they expect to stay the way they are. But if Christianity is about anything at all, it is about people being changed.

Peter, Jesus' friend, is a case in point. When he met Jesus he was a headstrong youngster, wildly impulsive and with a roller-coaster spiritual life of spectacular ups and downs. But Jesus saw in Peter's extravagant enthusiasm a chance to build something strong, stable and dependable. It would take time. It would sometimes be painful. But it would come to pass. So Jesus renamed him 'Rock'.

There followed lavish assertions of faith, followed by equally lavish denials. There were rebukes and corrections, warnings and promises till finally there was the nightmare of the cross then disillusionment, doubt and betrayal. Peter, the would-be preacher and fisher of men, went back to his fishing boat and being the leader he was, he took the rest of Jesus' disenchanted team with him.

But then things changed. The news filtered through – unbelievable at first – that the tomb of Jesus was empty. Peter and John ran to see for themselves and at that point John was convinced that Jesus was risen. For Peter there had to be a personal meeting, probably because of unfinished business over his denial of his Lord.

Peter was never the same again. In a matter of weeks the man who had quailed before a little servant girl now took on the combined might of religious and political officialdom and proclaimed the Gospel of the risen Christ without fear. Like an unquenchable flame Peter blazed for the rest of his days through the Roman Empire. Until, if tradition be correct, he met his death in the persecutions of the Emperor Nero.

Peter, the Rock, was wonderfully changed. Our natures are the same as Peter's, but then we also have the same Lord. We too can be forgiven, liberated and made new. We too can be set free from those things that have hindered us from becoming what Jesus knows we could be. We too can be changed.

Prayer:

O Lord Jesus, changer of men and women, please set us free from those things that have hampered our likeness to you and which have prevented us from being what we should be. Amen.

32

Reliable reality

Many have undertaken to draw up an account of the things that have been fulfilled among us, just as they were handed down to us by those who from the first were eyewitnesses and servants of the word. Therefore, since I myself have carefully investigated everything from the beginning, it seemed good also to me to write an orderly account for you, most excellent Theophilus, so that you may know the certainty of the things you have been taught.

(Luke 1:1–4)

● ● ●

If you are inclined to write off the Bible as a collection of fairy tales, I challenge you to study the Gospel of Luke. Luke is a self-confessed historian and he invites us to look closely at what he has written and see whether or not it holds water. He wants his readers to 'know the certainty of the things you have been taught'.

Luke wants us to be sure of the historical reliability of the Greatest Story Ever Told. He sets his account squarely in the context of Roman Imperial history. For example John the Baptist, a relative and a forerunner of Jesus, began his ministry in the fifteenth year of Tiberias Caesar when Pontius Pilate was Governor of Judea, Herod was Tetrarch of Galilee, his brother Philip was

Tetrarch of Ituraea and Trachonitus, during the High Priesthood of Annas and Caiaphas. Does that sound like someone writing a fairy tale? Here are historical people for the archaeologist or the historian to check and in each case investigations have proved Luke to be an accurate historian.

Arthur Thompson, an Australian archaeologist, says 'Luke is shown to be a most careful recorder of information, whether it be matters of geography and political boundaries, local customs, titles of local officers, local and religious practices, details of local topography, or the disposition of buildings in Greek or Roman or Asian or European towns'.

Sir William Ramsay, at one time Professor of History at St Andrew's University in Scotland, having spent many years studying Luke's writings concluded that 'Luke is a historian of the first rank' and that he should be 'placed along with the very greatest of historians'. Professor Blaiklock, at one time Professor of Classics at Auckland University, New Zealand, claims that Luke was 'a consummate historian, to be ranged in his own right with the great writers of the Greeks'.

If, in every place where Luke can be checked he is found to be accurate, can we not also trust him in those instances where he cannot be checked? Having told the truth so accurately so often is he likely to be less reliable at other times? Why should we doubt what he has to say about the words and deeds of the remarkable person who is the subject of his book? Why should we not accept his reports of the numerous encounters that the Apostles had with the risen Christ? Why should we not put our trust in the Christ that Luke knew and trusted?

Prayer:

Dear Heavenly Father, we are grateful for the reliability of the Scriptures that you have given us. Help us to share the good things written in them with the people of our own time. For Jesus' sake. Amen.

Getting out of the ghetto

The eye cannot say to the hand, 'I don't need you!'
And the head cannot say to the feet, 'I don't need
you!' On the contrary, those parts of the body that
seem to be weaker are indispensable, and the parts
that we think are less honourable we treat with
special honour. And the parts that are unpresentable
are treated with special modesty, while our
presentable parts need no special treatment. But
God has combined the members of the body and
has given greater honour to the parts that lacked it,
so that there should be no division in the body, but
that its parts should have equal concern for each
other. If one part suffers, every part suffers with it; if
one part is honoured, every part rejoices with it.
Now you are the body of Christ, and each one of
you is a part of it.

(I Corinthians 12:21–27)

●●●

An Anglican and a Baptist were arguing about the
respective merits of their different denominations.
After almost coming to blows the Anglican said 'I
don't know what we are fighting about. We are both
doing the Lord's work – you in your way and we in
his!' Most of us would not be so crass as to put it
this way, I suppose, but if we are honest it may be
how we sometimes think and feel. And when
denominationalism looms that large in our minds it

gives me some sympathy with the Sunday school child who asked her friend 'What's your abomination?'

Denominationalism sometimes bases itself on various doctrinal issues and this appears to give it a certain respectability – we are 'fighting for the truth'. They may be important but if we become fixated on such things and make them the criterion for acceptance of Christians who have a different point of view, it can easily centralise the peripheral. It was a wise Baptist who, when asked how he felt about adult baptism by immersion, replied 'It's fine, but you mustn't hang around the river too long'.

Sometimes denominationalism is simply fuelled by such unworthy things as pride, party-spirit and competition. We need to be very honest with ourselves about this. We will sometimes need to strip off a religious veneer so as to expose the murky motives that lie beneath our pious declarations.

Our fundamental unity in Christ, regardless of denomination or race, came home to me with refreshing joy one day in Johannesburg. I was standing at a busy pedestrian intersection when, above the traffic din, I heard a shout, 'Mojalifa!' (my African name). I turned and saw in the lofty cabin of a coal truck, a beaming, but unknown to me, African face. I dodged into the traffic and grabbed his outstretched hand. 'Allelujah' I cried and 'praise JEE-SAS' he shouted back. And then as the light turned green I had to jump for it. But it was a jump for joy because, as I went on my way I saw afresh how all our silly artificial barriers had just melted away amid the roar of the traffic.

Prayer:

Dear Lord Jesus, help us to keep our eyes focused on you and not on our differences. Save us from making our own denomination's 'household rules' a barrier to fellowship with your other disciples. Amen.

34

No check-mate

Some sat in darkness and the deepest gloom, prisoners suffering in iron chains, for they had rebelled against the words of God and despised the counsel of the Most High. So he subjected them to bitter labour; they stumbled, and there was no one to help. Then they cried to the LORD in their trouble, and he saved them from their distress. He brought them out of darkness and the deepest gloom and broke away their chains. Let them give thanks to the LORD for his unfailing love and his wonderful deeds for men, for he breaks down gates of bronze and cuts through bars of iron.

(Psalm 107:10–16)

●●●

In a famous German poem Faust, the main character, sells his soul to the devil in order to gain power and knowledge. The poem written by Johann Wolfgang von Goethe, later became the subject of a painting. In it Faust and Satan are playing a game of chess. The game is almost over and Faust has only a few pieces left – his king, a knight and a couple of pawns. On his face is a look of despair and the devil looks on gloatingly. It is checkmate. 'Mankind is outwitted by the powers of darkness.'

Most chess players have looked at the picture and agreed that the position was hopeless. It was checkmate. The devil had won. But one day a great master of the game came to the gallery and studied the picture. People came and went. The master stood and gazed at the picture. Suddenly the gallery echoed with his great and triumphant shout: 'It is a lie. It is a lie. The king and the knight have another move!'

Life can be like a lost chess game. It can seem to be so full of deadlocks. We try one way out after another but find ourselves in a *cul-de-sac*. The powers of the world, the flesh and the devil seem to hedge us in and prevent escape. We are stymied. It is check-mate.

But that is only the human perspective. Let God into the picture and immediately in the gallery of life there is a triumphant shout: 'It is a lie. The King has another move!' While Christ is on the scene there is another move.

During a mission up in the Vaal Triangle, South Africa, our team was involved in counselling people with a tremendous range of needs. There were parents whose kids had gone haywire. There was an elderly lady whose son-in-law wanted her dead so that he could get at her money. There were marital deadlocks and everywhere we turned there were people who were check-mated. Like some despairing Faust they were hemmed in by an inexplicable fear, unshakable guilt, irreconcilable relationship, or irreparable emotional scar. But, as we counselled them, it was clear that God had a way out for them, some other move which put a whole new angle on their situation.

I do not know what *cul-de-sac* you find yourself in today. I do not know what has you check-mated. I only know that against the sombre backdrop of your bad news is the bright shining light of God's good news, the Gospel of our Lord Jesus Christ. It is not check-mate. There is another move. The King will lead you into it and finish the game with a shout of victory.

Prayer:
O God, please do not leave us boxed in by those things that have kept us sad and defeated. Help us to realise that with you there is hope, the situation is never in check-mate. Amen.

35

A Christian Africa

Now an angel of the Lord said to Philip, 'Go south to the road – the desert road – that goes down from Jerusalem to Gaza.' So he started out, and on his way he met an Ethiopian eunuch, an important official in charge of all the treasury of Candace, queen of the Ethiopians. This man had gone to Jerusalem to worship, and on his way home was sitting in his chariot reading the book of Isaiah the prophet. The Spirit told Philip, 'Go to that chariot and stay near it.' Then Philip ran up to the chariot and heard the man reading Isaiah the prophet. 'Do you understand what you are reading?' Philip asked. 'How can I,' he said, 'unless someone explains it to me?' So he invited Philip to come up and sit with him. The eunuch was reading this passage of Scripture: 'He was led like a sheep to the slaughter, and as a lamb before the shearer is silent, so he did not open his mouth. In his humiliation he was deprived of justice. Who can speak of his descendants? For his life was taken from the earth.' The eunuch asked Philip, 'Tell me, please, who is the prophet talking about, himself or someone else?' Then Philip began with that very passage of Scripture and told him the good news about Jesus.

(Acts 8:26–35)

●●●

Most of the news about Africa is pretty dismal.

There is political chaos and confusion; there is murder and mayhem; there is economic disaster. For many, the so-called 'Dark Continent' seems to be getting darker.

What we do not hear in the news is the phenomenal growth of Christianity in Africa. According to Dr David Barrett, a leading Christian statistician, the total number of Christians (Protestant, Catholic, Orthodox, Coptic and Independent), will be about 350 million by the turn of the century, that is 60% of the continent's population. No other continent, not even Latin America, can compare with this. With the church in Europe and America under threat, perhaps it is Africa that will save the day.

Part of the growth in Africa is from natural birth. But a greater increase comes through the sterling work of catechists, missionaries and other lay people. By the year AD 2000 the centre of gravity of the Christian world will have shifted from the Northern Hemisphere to the Southern Hemisphere (Africa and Latin America). The 'younger' churches of the Third World will have multiplied seventeen times from 67 million in 1900 to over one billion in the year 2000.

Will the missionary initiative of the Christian church at large be taken up by Africa and Latin America while Western Christendom staggers from crisis to crisis, hampered by its theological compromises and institutionalism? While Africa is busy preaching a personal, living, resurrected Jesus who changes and revolutionises lives, the Western church may well be hampered by ideology and methodology.

Some of Jesus' first words would have been

spoken in Africa (Matthew 2:13) and when he made his way to Calvary it was an African who helped to carry the cross (Matthew 27:32). Jesus must have a special place in his heart for Africa. The question is – do we?

Prayer:
Lord, we are very glad to hear how the Good News of Jesus is moving so rapidly through Africa. Empower those who preach it, remove all obstacles to it, and prosper its expansion throughout the African continent. For Jesus' sake. Amen.

36

The prodigal's principle

When he came to his senses, he said, 'How many of my father's hired men have food to spare, and here I am starving to death! I will set out and go back to my father and say to him: Father, I have sinned against heaven and against you. I am no longer worthy to be called your son; make me like one of your hired men.' So he got up and went to his father. But while he was still a long way off, his father saw him and was filled with compassion for him; he ran to his son, threw his arms around him and kissed him. The son said to him, 'Father, I have sinned against heaven and against you. I am no longer worthy to be called your son.' But the father said to his servants, 'Quick! Bring the best robe and put it on him. Put a ring on his finger and sandals on his feet. Bring the fattened calf and kill it. Let's have a feast and celebrate. For this son of mine was dead and is alive again; he was lost and is found.'

(Luke 15:17–24)

●●●

As a teenager I often thought how much happier I would feel on the Isle of Capri or the French Riviera. I thought I would feel different in a new situation, especially a romantic one. These days I travel a lot and I meet people who have a similar outlook. Travel and tourism have become a form of escape. However I have found that when I travel I

take myself with me. Changing places does not change me nor anyone else either and the grass is not greener on the other side. If we cannot live with ourselves where we are now, we will find ourselves equally intolerable anywhere else.

We have to live with ourselves, warts and all, and that makes it so important for us to become 'livable-with'. This means motivation to change the changeable, resignation to accept the unchangeable and discernment to know which is which. With my third-rate voice I will never sing opera – I cannot change that. But if I have a first-rate temper or king-size complex, something must be done about that.

The prodigal son in Jesus' famous story first 'came to himself' before he came home to his father. He discovered that the grass of the far country was actually brown rather than green. The problem was not the place, it was the person – himself and when he discovered this he was able to set out for home and reconciliation with his father. The process of personal change through Christian conversion begins with the same realisation: that things are not right with us and that something needs to be done about it.

The next step is to see how marvellously God has acted to clear the barriers so that he can give us the best of all home-comings. When his Son died for us on the cross he made it possible for us, now aware of our need of forgiveness and reconciliation, to come to him and enjoy forever the warmth of his love and acceptance.

'He came to himself … and he came to his father'. From guilt to grace – this is the way of change.

Prayer:

Father, we know that you wait for us to come home from the far country of sin and selfishness. We know that, despite the past, Jesus has made it possible for us to be accepted just as we are. Take us in, change us and use us in your service. Amen.

37

God in a box

Praise the Lord, O my soul. O Lord my God, you are very great; you are clothed with splendour and majesty. He wraps himself in light as with a garment; he stretches out the heavens like a tent and lays the beams of his upper chambers on their waters. He makes the clouds his chariot and rides on the wings of the wind. He makes winds his messengers, flames of fire his servants. He set the earth on its foundations; it can never be moved. You covered it with the deep as with a garment; the waters stood above the mountains. But at your rebuke the waters fled, at the sound of your thunder they took to flight; they flowed over the mountains, they went down into the valleys, to the place you assigned for them. You set a boundary they cannot cross; never again will they cover the earth.

(Psalm 104:1–9)

●●●

At school we irreverently called the chapel the 'God-box'. To us, in those far off days, the chapel building was the box where God was neatly confined within its walls. If we wanted to find him or talk to him that was the place to go. He was there where he was safe. I don't know what would have happened if he had broken out of the box and invaded the classroom, the football field or the dormitory.

It is not only children who put God in a box. Many adults also visualise him within some constricted conceptual framework. Perhaps he is an Ancient with a proverbial white beard or a genial cosmic Santa Claus. In fact I believe that boxing God in, whether physically or conceptually, is one of our favourite and most disastrous adult games. It may be a denominational box or one made out of our own pet theories about him. Perhaps it is a reinforced strong-box made from our special theological or ecclesiastical biases.

Take the person of Jesus for example. Some leave him sitting on one of those little chairs in the Sunday School to be the innocuous friend of little children. Others send him to the lecture room for amputation, modification and updating (this box is often constructed in the shape of a coffin). In recent times some have sent him off to join a revolutionary army to be one of God's guerillas fighting to liberate the oppressed. Whatever way the box is made, it always succeeds in keeping God out of the way and free from interfering in our lives.

This is why studying the Jesus of the New Testament is so disturbing. That is why walking with him through life is so profoundly challenging and yet such radical fun. We discover that he can never be confined, summarised, categorised or simply filed under 'J for Jesus'. He is forever breaking out of our mental boxes bringing solace to the suffering, strength to the living, hope to the dying. He loves both the oppressor and the oppressed, the child and the genius. Like those who went to his tomb on Easter Day we discover afresh that 'He is not here: he is risen'.

Prayer:

Dear Heavenly Father, please forgive us for our small-mindedness in thinking about you. We have too often reduced you to the tiny dimensions of our own thought and action. Please help us to get as big a picture of you and your Son, Jesus, as our small brains can manage. Amen.

38

The history mystery

So Joseph also went up from the town of Nazareth in Galilee to Judea, to Bethlehem the town of David, because he belonged to the house and line of David. He went there to register with Mary, who was pledged to be married to him and was expecting a child. While they were there, the time came for the baby to be born, and she gave birth to her firstborn, a son. She wrapped him in cloths and placed him in a manger, because there was no room for them in the inn. And there were shepherds living out in the fields nearby, keeping watch over their flocks at night. An angel of the Lord appeared to them, and the glory of the Lord shone around them, and they were terrified. But the angel said to them, 'Do not be afraid. I bring you good news of great joy that will be for all the people. Today in the town of David a Saviour has been born to you; he is Christ the Lord. This will be a sign to you: You will find a baby wrapped in cloths and lying in a manger.' Suddenly a great company of the heavenly host appeared with the angel, praising God and saying, 'Glory to God in the highest, and on earth peace to men on whom his favour rests.'

(Luke 2:4–14)

●●●

History does not always seem to make a lot of sense. It seems to be the account of humanity stumbling from one crisis to another. Is it going somewhere? Well, let's pick up a Bible (which has a lot of history in it) and see if we can find some clues.

About 1900 BC a man called Abraham, a resident of the city of Ur in Mesopotamia, got a disturbing message from God. If he would set out with God he would be given a land, descendants and his obedience would bring blessing to the whole world. So he set out for Canaan, then occupied by warlike tribes and as unlikely as it might have seemed, God assured him that his descendants would someday possess this promised land.

When, in the course of time, his descendants became slaves in Egypt this promise must have seemed even more unlikely. However, one of the great escapes of all time eventually had them again *en route* for Canaan and its eventual conquest. In due course, for political unity they adopted a monarchy, which was a mixed blessing and which eventually split them into kingdoms, Israel in the North and Judah in the South.

Spiritual rebellion saw the North obliterated by the Assyrians and the South carried captive by the Babylonians. But once again their sovereign God brought Judah back again to its ruined city and temple and life moved on again. Empires rose and fell, the Greeks, the Persians and then the Romans who brought a measure of political stability to the whole world.

Suddenly the veil of heaven was rent and the explanation to the history mystery invaded our world. Or as St Paul explained it 'when the time had fully come, God sent his Son'. At last the age old promise to Abraham was completely fulfilled and humanity's true King and Saviour had come.

So history is not out of control. It is moving steadily to its culmination. And for us that means the return of our Lord Jesus Christ in power and great glory.

Prayer:
Father, we are encouraged to know that the true story of the world is not made up of the mess that we see in our newspapers and the chaos that we hear about on the radio. In Jesus history has a meaning, a purpose and a wonderful conclusion. Help us to see that and not to despair. For Jesus' sake. Amen.

39

Arrival ... what then?

People who want to get rich fall into temptation and a trap and into many foolish and harmful desires that plunge men into ruin and destruction. For the love of money is a root of all kinds of evil. Some people, eager for money, have wandered from the faith and pierced themselves with many griefs. But you, man of God, flee from all this, and pursue righteousness, godliness, faith, love, endurance and gentleness. Fight the good fight of the faith. Take hold of the eternal life to which you were called when you made your good confession in the presence of many witnesses. In the sight of God, who gives life to everything, and of Christ Jesus, who while testifying before Pontius Pilate made the good confession, I charge you to keep this command without spot or blame until the appearing of our Lord Jesus Christ, which God will bring about in his own time – God, the blessed and only Ruler, the King of kings and Lord of lords.

(I Timothy 6:9–15)

●●●

The French language, with its characteristic incisiveness has an excellent word for a go-getter. It calls such a person *un arriviste* – an arrivist. I suppose we are all trying to go places and arrive. The big question is: where?

For many the summit is social success. These are

the climbers who strive to know the right people, throw the right parties, go to the right schools and universities and – if they get involved in charity work – get their picture in the right magazines. Their motivation seems to be recognition, perhaps even praise, from others. A woman I once knew worked so hard at this that she was finally so bored she had a nervous breakdown.

Another goal is financial success and a lot of modern idolatry focuses on this golden lollipop of wealth. If social climbing makes us feel important because of whom we know and mix with, the money-tree climber sees his or her value in what they possess. Both points of view deny what is our real human value – that we are made in the image of God, not the golden calf.

The Bible bids us be content with what we have and assures those who trust in Christ that God will never leave them or forsake them. Of course we all have to deal with money and be responsible in the use of it, but loving the stuff is another matter. It is like a drug which has the power to alter our consciousness and give distorted visions of the world.

What is the point of having the best of everything in houses and cars and gadgets or being invited to the best parties or getting our names in *Who's Who,* if finally we enter eternity stripped of all these things and stand on equal terms alongside the most destitute person on earth? We will all be called eventually to give an account of ourselves.

Jesus told a chilling story of a wealthy landowner who did so well financially that he decided to re-invest and then indulge himself with high living. In the story God calls him a fool because the day that he decided these things was his last day on earth.

Jesus on the cross looked to be the world's biggest failure, the supreme non-arrivist. But what he did for us there pulls the stuffing out of all our crazy self-congratulation. Before the cross we stand naked, stripped of everything but the grace and mercy of God. If we must arrive somewhere that is the place to be.

Prayer:
Lord Jesus, nothing in my hand I bring, simply to your cross I cling. Amen.

40

Springtime in Autumn

We know that the one who raised the Lord Jesus from the dead will also raise us with Jesus and present us with you in his presence. All this is for your benefit, so that the grace that is reaching more and more people may cause thanksgiving to overflow to the glory of God. Therefore we do not lose heart. Though outwardly we are wasting away, yet inwardly we are being renewed day by day. For our light and momentary troubles are achieving for us an eternal glory that far outweighs them all. So we fix our eyes not on what is seen, but on what is unseen. For what is seen is temporary, but what is unseen is eternal. Now we know that if the earthly tent we live in is destroyed, we have a building from God, an eternal house in heaven, not built by human hands.

(2 Corinthians 4:14–5:1)

•••

The changing of the seasons has always fascinated people. They featured in Shakespeare's sonnets of life and love and Vivaldi wrote beautiful music about them. The seasons dictate the farmer's routine and rearrange our sporting fixtures. They are God's time-piece and calendar which guarantees for us the regularity of the universe.

But what of the seasons of life? Perhaps we recognise in the year's changes a similar pattern to our own experience. We go from the spring of adolescence to the summer of adulthood and then to the autumn of the middle years and the winter of old age.We find ourselves in flux, in growth and in decay. But what is the end of it all? Does the drama of life end in meaninglessness and the grave? Is the last rose of summer really the last or could life's winter be followed by another spring?

For some this process points to disillusionment and despair. For others it involves a desperate attempt, through pumping iron, and swallowing vitamins to stave off the inevitable end. H.G. Wells said, 'Unless there is a more abundant life before mankind, this scheme of space and time is a bad joke – an empty laugh braying across the mysteries'.

The Gospel of Christ challenges this sad picture. It assures us that for humanity, unlike nature, there can be springtime in autumn (or in summer and winter too). A Professor who turned to Christ when over 80 said 'I'm but a little child; my life has just begun'. The outward person does indeed suffer wear and tear and eventually falls into death and decay. But in Christ there is a perpetual springtime, a constant rejuvenation of the spirit. In Christ the end of life is but the beginning of new life, the glorious dawn that comes after the shades of night have fallen. When the Gospel is offered and received, spring-fever is in the air.

Prayer:
Father, I am glad to know that, as the years pass and my body starts to run down, you are at work within me, renewing, refreshing, restoring and renovating and that, at the end, you will re-make me into the very likeness of Jesus. Amen.

41

A letter from Mrs Pilate

While Pilate was sitting on the judge's seat, his wife sent him this message: 'Don't have anything to do with that innocent man, for I have suffered a great deal today in a dream because of him.' But the chief priests and the elders persuaded the crowd to ask for Barabbas and to have Jesus executed. 'Which of the two do you want me to release to you?' asked the governor. 'Barabbas,' they answered. 'What shall I do, then, with Jesus who is called Christ?' Pilate asked. They all answered, 'Crucify him!' 'Why? What crime has he committed?' asked Pilate. But they shouted all the louder, 'Crucify him!' When Pilate saw that he was getting nowhere, but that instead an uproar was starting, he took water and washed his hands in front of the crowd. 'I am innocent of this man's blood,' he said. 'It is your responsibility!'

(Matthew 27:19–24)

●●●

Dear Pontius

I have been so worried that I just had to send you this note. It is about that trial – there is something pretty scary about it. For one thing you know that the previous trial by the religious leaders was illegal. What if Tiberius hears about it? You are in trouble enough already and this would be the end of all your chances of promotion.

Also, my dear, Festus told me privately that you

did not seem to be yourself during your examination of the prisoner Jesus. Festus says that the prisoner seemed to take the initiative from you when he spoke to you about his claims for himself. It looked like you were the one on trial.

I wish you had listened to my dream. I know you think I am superstitious but the dream was so vivid that it almost seemed to be a message to us from someone. The Jewish God perhaps? In the dream I saw this Jesus as being innocent and good and rather god-like. But you handed him over to that snarling pack and I wept and wept for you – and then I woke up. What if my dream was a warning?

I understand that you were unnerved by the prisoner's mention of 'truth'. Why? Are you afraid of the truth? Perhaps this Jesus knows more about that subject than we do. I sometimes think that despite all the glorious achievements of the Empire we have not found any good answers to the real riddles of life: Why are we here? What happens after death? Is it possible to communicate with God?

If the mob has their way they will cart him off to be crucified and we will never know whether or not we have missed out on a solution to the mysteries of existence. I know you think I'm silly when I talk like this but the whole thing has made me very anxious.

You know I never interfere with your official business. But I want our children to remember you as a great and wise Governor who was always just and fair and who always made the right decisions about people. I would hate to think that you might go down in history as the man who murdered the Truth. Wouldn't it be awful if somehow this Jesus came back from the dead and people, in the future, spoke about him as one who 'suffered under Pontius

Pilate'. I know it doesn't sound very likely but you never can tell …

Pontius come home as early as you can. Could we not go to Caesarea for the weekend?

Lovingly

Claudia

Prayer:

Loving Heavenly Father, we are so grateful that when Jesus went to his trial he put the whole world on trial and then went to the cross to pay the penalty for us all. Thank you. Amen.

42

Wanted: A revival

*When Solomon had finished the temple of the Lord
and the royal palace, and had succeeded in carrying
out all he had in mind to do in the temple of the
Lord and in his own palace, the Lord appeared to
him at night and said:*
*'I have heard your prayer and have chosen this
place for myself as a temple for sacrifices.*
*'When I shut up the heavens so that there is no
rain, or command locusts to devour the land or send
a plague among my people, if my people, who are
called by my name, will humble themselves and pray
and seek my face and turn from their wicked ways,
then will I hear from heaven and will forgive their
sin and will heal their land.'*

(2 Chronicles 7:11–14)

● ● ●

I am not a politician but I have spent a fair bit of
time talking to politicians. In the bad old days before
the end of *Apartheid* we often did what we could in
discussions with some of them about the much-
needed changes in South Africa. Our *Kolobe Lodge*
events were also very exciting as we took politicians
away for a weekend of fun and mutual
understanding (you can read about this in my book
A witness for ever). When I am overseas I am often
called upon to speak to parliamentary gatherings.

However, when it comes to real change I have

long despaired of finding satisfactory political solutions. I am sure that the answer is found in spiritual revival such as the 18th century Wesleyan re-awakening in England.

England had been in a mess. There was moral and spiritual depression and there was much unrest. Political life was dominated by ecclesiastical parties and bitterness was widespread. The Episcopalians and the non-conformists were locked in controversy. Watching this made the nation sceptical of religion and soon reason was enthroned as the new goddess. The historian Gibbon says that morality in the universities was at an all time low. Another historian wrote that 'of prominent statesmen of the time the greater part were distinguished for the grossness and immorality of their lives'.

There was much violence in the land and although the death sentence could be imposed for stealing a sheep or cutting down a cherry tree, little children were kept in the mines for 12 hours a day. It was a grim and unhappy time and the cry by those who still prayed was for God to send England better things.

Then John and Charles Wesley and their itinerants burst on the scene preaching the everlasting Gospel openly in streets and fields. As the Good News sounded forth, poor tired old England took a turn for the better. People went back to the Bible, there was music and laughter in the air and soon much-needed reforms began to emerge. The evil of slavery was dealt with along with the pitiful conditions in prisons and mines. Many historians believe that the Wesleyan Revival saved England from the blood-letting of the French Revolution.

This is history. This happened. And the God of history can make it happen again. Politics is necessary and we should pray for those who are called to engage in it. But for deep and lasting change we must dig deeper than politics. We must penetrate the hearts and minds of men and women and save them from themselves with the power of the everlasting Gospel. Pray for it. Others did and look what happened.

Prayer:
O God, send us revival and begin it in me. Amen.

43

The rat race

*Then he (Jesus) called the crowd to him along with
his disciples and said: 'If anyone would come after
me, he must deny himself and take up his cross and
follow me. For whoever wants to save his life will
lose it, but whoever loses his life for me and for the
gospel will save it. What good is it for a man to gain
the whole world, yet forfeit his soul? Or what can a
man give in exchange for his soul?'*

(Mark 8:34–37)

●●●

'On your marks! Get set! Go!' cried the
kindergarten teacher and the rat-race was on. Buro
(short for Bureaucrat) and Pluto (short for Plutocrat)
were willing competitors, glad to get into the race
early in life. The teacher was convinced that the way
to get the best out of her little charges was to foster
cut-throat competition. And this was not hard to do
because B and P were just as ambitious and
competitive as little human beings might have been.
They fought it out again in high school and
university, jostling for popularity, position and
power. Each of them formed their own pressure
groups, Buro doing it with memos and manifestos,
Pluto with the judicious use of money.

As they made their way into the big world Buro
went into government service and Pluto stepped into
his father's company and quickly got into the race

for the top. Buro laughed long and hard every time he was able to complicate matters for Pluto and Co by requiring more forms for them to complete in quadruplicate. As they continued to strive with each other, their blood pressure went through the roof and from time to time they asked themselves whether the contest was worth the effort.

They both sat on endless committees and agendas and budgets proliferated until life's pleasures were crushed under the weight. They tried vitamins, tranquillisers and workouts at the gym. Buro now rated a driver to relieve him from battling with the traffic; Pluto came to work an hour later so as to miss the rush hour. But although they were both 'successful' neither seemed to be enjoying it much.

Eventually Buro became Receiver of Revenue and Pluto made it to Managing Director. But for both the stress and strain of the years took their toll and each died in action – Buro while drawing up more canny and complicated tax forms and Pluto in a desperate effort to evade their demands. Buro died suddenly of *papyrioma pleroma* (an excess of paper) and Pluto choked on the olive in his martini as he read his tax bill.

All agreed that they were noble runners in the rat-race. But don't ask me who won. Maybe after death a more Reliable Judge with a different perspective will shed more light on the subject.

Prayer:
Father, save us from 'success' if such a thing means running and running and running without getting nearer to you or to others. For Jesus' sake. Amen.

44

V for Victory

I will not boast about myself, except about my weaknesses. Even if I should choose to boast, I would not be a fool, because I would be speaking the truth. But I refrain, so no-one will think more of me than is warranted by what I do or say. To keep me from becoming conceited because of these surpassingly great revelations, there was given me a thorn in my flesh, a messenger of Satan, to torment me. Three times I pleaded with the Lord to take it away from me. But he said to me, 'My grace is sufficient for you, for my power is made perfect in weakness.' Therefore I will boast all the more gladly about my weaknesses, so that Christ's power may rest on me. (2 Corinthians 12:5–9)

●●●

Although I was only a child in 1945, I remember the excitement of VE Day – Victory in Europe! After so much death and despair it came like the rising of the sun after a dark night. Victory! No more war. People coming home. What a Day!

'Victory' is a great word but not used much these days. Many people feel defeated rather than victorious, beaten by temptation, fractured personal relationships and a sense of meaninglessness in life.

The fact that the Bible does not mean us to live this way came home to me with great force at an informal meeting in our church. A young woman, who sensed that I seemed weary and depressed, said: "I feel that God wants me to refer Michael to a promise in Isaiah (41:10) which reads 'do not fear, for I am with you; do not be dismayed, for I am your God. I will strengthen you and help you; I will uphold you with my victorious right hand".

What a wonderful promise, especially as I was just about to embark on some exacting days of ministry in Johannesburg for which I felt very inadequate. I needed strength to overcome my weakness and here was God's promise that he would supply it. However when I opened the Bible what struck me with considerable force was the word 'victorious'. It seemed to say to me that the hand that would hold me up in the days to come was not a weak or fumbling one but a victorious one.

When I phoned the young woman to thank her she said that she, too, on her way home from church had come to the same conviction that the key word in the promise was 'victorious'. So as I went to my meetings in Johannesburg, I lived on the assurance of this great promise and God fulfilled it wonderfully for me. I experienced times of joy and happiness and achievement and yes, of victory.

Perhaps the key to such an experience is what came before it – my sense of weakness and inability. God will fulfill his great promises to us, he will uphold us with his victorious hand but first we need to recognise that we cannot make it on our own.

Prayer:
O Lord, without you we are lost and weak and defeated. Help us to take our sense of helplessness to you so that you can infuse our defeated spirits with the victory of the cross. For Jesus' sake. Amen.

45

Whodunit?

*Now, brothers, I want to remind you of the gospel I
preached to you, which you received and on which
you have taken your stand. By this gospel you are
saved, if you hold firmly to the word I preached to
you. Otherwise, you have believed in vain. For what I
received I passed on to you as of first importance :
that Christ died for our sins according to the
Scriptures, that he was buried, that he was raised on
the third day according to the Scriptures, and that
he appeared to Peter, and then to the Twelve. After
that, he appeared to more than five hundred of the
brothers at the same time, most of whom are still
living, though some have fallen asleep. Then he
appeared to James, then to all the apostles, and last
of all he appeared to me also, as to one abnormally
born.*

(1 Corinthians 15: 1–8)

●●●

Do you like 'Whodunits'? Do you like exercising
your detective skills in solving a murder mystery?
Well, try yourself out on this one: who was
responsible for the disappearance of Jesus' body on
that first Easter Day?

First, a bit of reconstruction. On Friday, a man
considered by some to be a dangerous rabble-rouser,
was executed, certified dead by competent
executioners and buried in the tomb of a wealthy

nobleman. To prevent any trickery the local Governor had the tomb sealed and a guard mounted to protect it from interference by friend or foe.

The prisoner's followers, frightened and disillusioned, retreated into hiding. The political and religious authorities, after a heavy week, sighed with relief and looked forward to a quiet weekend.

But then it happened. The body was gone! Whodunit?

After a crisis meeting, the religious authorities bribed the soldiers to spread the rumour that while they were asleep on duty, (a crime usually punished by death in the Roman army), Jesus' disciples stole the body. Now, my good detective, please note: both friend and foe recognised the fact that the body was missing.

If the foes took it they would have simply been fostering a belief in the resurrection; all they would have had to do was produce the body and kill all speculation. If the friends removed the body the detective must deal with problems of morale, motivation and morality. Morale: they were hardly in a fit state to carry out such a daring raid. Motivation: what would they gain by it? Only ridicule, ostracism or even martyrdom. Morality: it seems absurd that Jesus' disciples would be part of a gigantic hoax. They preached and taught the highest ethic in all human history; could they have done that knowing that their account of a risen Messiah was a phoney story? And remember they held to their belief even in the face of torture and death.

The most convincing belief is that Jesus came forth from the tomb alive. And that means that he is still alive and ready to save. And it means there is hope – even for amateur detectives.

Prayer:

Dear Lord Jesus, risen and victorious Saviour, we thank you for the solid basis on which our faith in you rests. Please help us to commend it to others. Amen.

46

Following Dad's footsteps

*At that time the disciples came to Jesus and asked,
'Who is the greatest in the kingdom of heaven?'*
*He called a little child and had him stand among
them. And he said: 'I tell you the truth, unless you
change and become like little children, you will never
enter the kingdom of heaven. Therefore, whoever
humbles himself like this child is the greatest in the
kingdom of heaven.*
*'And whoever welcomes a little child like this in my
name welcomes me. But if anyone causes one of
these little ones who believe in me to sin, it would be
better for him to have a large millstone hung around
his neck and to be drowned in the depths of the
sea.'*   *(Matthew 18:1–6)*

•••

One crisp, snowy morning Hank J Hudson left
the warmth of home and made for his garaged car.
His new rubber overshoes made virgin tracks on the
fresh snow and his gloved hands fumbled with his
keys at the garage door. He heard a soft sound
behind him and turning saw his little five year old
coming towards him making long, strained strides so
as to step into the footprints in the snow.

'What are you doing, son?' asked Hank. 'I'm
stepping in Daddy's tracks' laughed the little boy.
Hank, too, was still laughing as he turned into the
Connecticut Turnpike for the daily commuter run

into the city. 'Stepping in Daddy's tracks', the words went round and round in his mind. 'It's a serious thing to have someone stepping in your tracks like that and that's what he is doing. He mimics me. It's sheer hero worship'.

The Hudson River passed beneath him. New York loomed larger and larger. 'Stepping in Daddy's tracks, that's what he's doing'. Hank reflected on what that could mean. Some doubtful business practices, a pedestrian and prosaic marriage, a bit of a moral slide. 'I don't want him to go that way' said Hank out loud to himself.

As he mused on this, a religious service that he had watched on TV came back to him. And so did the message, about Christ and receiving him into your life. Asking God for forgiveness. Following him and seeking, with his help, to live like a Christian.

When Hank arrived at his office he closed the door and knelt at his desk. 'Lord', he said, I could make a terrible hash of my life and I am on the way to doing it. And I have got that little chap stepping in my tracks. I want to be a Christian father and husband. I want to make good tracks that are worth stepping in. Lord, take over, forgive me my sins, I am going to follow you from now on'.

That night after he had told his wife, they both knelt and thanked God for the snowfalls of winter and the wisdom of children.

Prayer:
Dear Lord make me into the person that I ought to be and a proper example to others including those of my own family. I ask this in the name of Jesus who can make all things new. Amen.

47

Universe or multi-verse

And we pray this in order that you may live a life worthy of the Lord and may please him in every way: bearing fruit in every good work, growing in the knowledge of God, being strengthened with all power according to his glorious might so that you may have great endurance and patience, and joyfully giving thanks to the Father, who has qualified you to share in the inheritance of the saints in the kingdom of light. For he has rescued us from the dominion of darkness and brought us into the kingdom of the Son he loves, in whom we have redemption, the forgiveness of sins. He is the image of the invisible God, the firstborn over all creation. For by him all things were created: things in heaven and on earth, visible and invisible, whether thrones or powers or rulers or authorities; all things were created by him and for him. He is before all things, and in him all things hold together.

(Colossians 1:10–17)

●●●

Is the universe a whole, a unit, both physically, morally and spiritually? Or is it just a random collection of haphazard phenomena devoid of meaning, that is a multi-verse?

The word 'universe' comes from the Latin 'unus' (one) and 'versus' (turned), meaning something 'turned into one' or 'combined into one whole'. One dictionary defines it as being 'all created things viewed as constituting one system or whole'.

This suggests that everything is a cohesive whole, not a random, chaotic multi-verse. Despite the wisdom of the ages about this, we do not always view it in this way. We fail to see the moral and the spiritual as being one part with the physical and all established by the same Creator God. The Bible, as we might expect, presents all of life as a single piece, with Jesus Christ as the key to everything.

No doubt this fact came through loudly to those whose major reaction to Jesus was that he taught with 'authority'. When he spoke people immediately felt a sense of authenticity. They recognised that he was talking about reality, about things as they are, things which were in tune with their experience. When he claimed to be the Way and the Truth and the Life, he was obviously doing so with cosmic backing.

I believe that if we are honest we will see that values such as honesty, purity, kindness, forgiveness and reconciliation are undeniably creative. And we will see that evils such as dishonesty, immorality, jealousy, hatred, revenge and spiritual rebellion are destructive and disintegrative. In other words, what Jesus said about such things is backed by reality and we instinctively recognise it to be so. He is the Way to reality. He is the Truth at the heart of all things. He is the Life that is life indeed.

So if you want to go with the flow of the universe you must be on side with Christ. For things spiritual and things material came into being through him and they are sustained by him. He is the Alpha and the Omega, the first and the last – and all the bits in between.

Prayer:

Dear Lord Jesus, thank you for bringing us into contact with reality. In a world that lives on fantasy and fabrications, we stand with you on solid ground and find our place in your universe. Amen.

48

For God and my country

I urge, then, first of all, that requests, prayers, intercession and thanksgiving be made for everyone – for kings and all those in authority, that we may live peaceful and quiet lives in all godliness and holiness. This is good, and pleases God our Saviour, who wants all men to be saved and to come to a knowledge of the truth. For there is one God and one mediator between God and men, the man Christ Jesus, who gave himself as a ransom for all men – the testimony given in its proper time. And for this purpose I was appointed a herald and an apostle – I am telling the truth, I am not lying – and a teacher of the true faith to the Gentiles. I want men everywhere to lift up holy hands in prayer, without anger or disputing.   (1 Timothy 2:1–8)

●●●

'For God and My Country'. This is the motto of Uganda which we took as ours when our teams did a city-wide mission in Kampala in 1996. The Ugandans recognise that, as a nation, they have not succeeded so well in this, what with Idi Amin and Milton Obote and all the killings. But we sensed that there was a genuine desire to change and let God have his way in national life. As we focused on the leadership, political, professional, academic, business and military, we found the response quite remarkable.

Our approach was this: that the two loves, (God

and country) belong together and where they have not gone hand in hand, Africa has been plunged into two terrible perils. When there has been love of God without love of country, the Christian church has become pietistic and out of touch with the practical needs and problems of the nation. Society is then allowed to go to the dogs and the devil. Or sometimes, despite the piety, worldly values have invaded the church and it has become what one writer calls 'the nameless city set on the non-existent hill'.

The second peril arises when there is love for country but none for God or for the Christian ethic. Then there is godless nationalism and unprincipled government, where the blind lead the blind and both fall into the proverbial ditch. As the late Oginga Odinga of Kenya said 'we wasted thirty years of independence. We concentrated on power, wealth, personalities and tribes. And we forgot virtue'.

At our Kampala mission 'God and my country' was beautifully personified by the presence on the platform with us of the First Lady, Mrs Janet Museveni. She brought a very public and unashamed testimony to Jesus Christ as her personal Saviour and Lord and as the one whom the nation should follow. And she made it quite clear that if Jesus was to be important in Uganda he must be supremely important. Subsequently she and her husband bought a house and presented it to the nation as a 'house of prayer'.

Prayer:
Dear Heavenly Father, help us to be good Christians and good citizens so that we help to build a society in which lives can be enriched and transformed. For Jesus' sake. Amen.

49

Giving it a go

(Jesus said) 'Love your enemies, do good to them, and lend to them without expecting to get anything back. Then your reward will be great, and you will be sons of the Most High, because he is kind to the ungrateful and wicked. Be merciful, just as your Father is merciful.

'Do not judge, and you will not be judged. Do not condemn, and you will not be condemned. Forgive, and you will be forgiven. Give, and it will be given to you. A good measure, pressed down, shaken together and running over, will be poured into your lap. For with the measure you use, it will be measured to you.'

(Luke 6:35–38)

•••

There was great excitement in an Indian city for the Rajah of the province was to pass through. Amid the festivities was a beggar whose bowl was rapidly filled with rice by the crowds. 'I only get rice', lamented the beggar, 'but if I can catch the Rajah's eye he might give me gold'. When the great one arrived the beggar yelled, 'My bowl, my bowl, see my bowl. Out of your bounty and charity give me something!'

Stopping his gorgeously apparelled elephant the Rajah said to the beggar, 'You give me something first'.

The beggar was angry: how could he, a poor penniless creature, give anything to this fabulously rich man? With bad grace he put a single grain of rice into his bowl and handed it up to the Rajah who then handed it back. As the procession moved on the beggar sat in the dust weeping but then he saw in his bowl a piece of gold the size of a grain of rice.

'O fool, fool, fool that I am,' he wailed, 'If only I had given all I had'.

Life is a lot like that. We get out of it what we put in. We either get from life a few tiny nuggets, crumbs from the table of meaningful existence, or else we give it all we've got and find ourselves curiously exhilarated. We become rich in fulfilment and we benefit others as well as ourselves.

We should give all we've got as spouses and parents till our marriages sparkle and our children thrive and flourish. We should give our all to our communities and nations and become catalysts in nation building.

But nowhere is this principle more important than in our spiritual lives. Give Christ a small grain of our existence, and because he is generous, he will give us a nugget back. But give him all and the return is lavish and abundant.

Jesus said 'it is more blessed to give than to receive'. That is not just a pretty idea, it is a law of life. A Greek shipping magnate challenged by a friend of mine asked, 'Would Jesus like me to give him a ship?' My friend replied, 'I don't think so. He wants you to give him yourself. But then he knows that if he gets you he gets all your ships'.

Come on, fellow beggars. Let's give Jesus the whole bowl!

Prayer:

Please Lord take me and all I've got, my time, talents and possessions. Help me to 'let go and let God' and make myself rich in the experience of life. For Jesus' sake. Amen.

50

The cradle way

After the Sabbath, at dawn on the first day of the week, Mary Magdalene and the other Mary went to look at the tomb. There was a violent earthquake, for an angel of the Lord came down from heaven and, going to the tomb, rolled back the stone and sat on it. His appearance was like lightning, and his clothes were white as snow. The guards were so afraid of him that they shook and became like dead men. The angel said to the women, "Do not be afraid, for I know that you are looking for Jesus, who was crucified. He is not here; he has risen, just as he said. Come and see the place where he lay. Then go quickly and tell his disciples: 'He has risen from the dead and is going ahead of you into Galilee. There you will see him.' Now I have told you." So the women hurried away from the tomb, afraid yet filled with joy, and ran to tell his disciples.

(Matthew 28:1–8)

• • •

When I visited Bethlehem what struck me most was how small it was, how apparently insignificant. I was reminded that when the Son of God slipped quietly into history he did not come in a chariot of fire accompanied by legions of angels. He came via the body of a humble Hebrew maiden.

Fay Inchfawn, in her poem *The Cradle Way*, catches something of the wonder of Jesus' birth and what his life has meant for womankind:

> God comes to men in flame of fire: In rushing winds
> or fierce desire:
> In light, all blinding and intense: in thunderings of
> Omnipotence.
> But to a woman's heart he comes not with the beat
> and blare of drums:
> Nor with the shriek of trumpets, nay! He enters by
> – the Cradle Way.
> Through woman Adam was unmanned, yet by her
> God Almighty planned;
> Because he knew this thing was true, her heart was
> greater than her hand.
> T'was woman's hands that did prepare the King of
> Glory's earthly wear.
> A tremulous woman who uprose and wrapped him
> round with swaddling clothes.
> It was a woman's arm that crept about God's
> Darling as he slept.
> And here lies woman's right to fame: to her the first
> sweet Christian came.

Dorothy Sayers wrote in the same vein: 'perhaps
it is no wonder that women were first at the cradle
and last at the cross. They had never known a man
like this man – there never has been another such. A
prophet and a teacher who never nagged at them.
Never flattered or coaxed or patronised … who
never mapped out their sphere for them; never
urged them to be feminine or jeered at them for
being female; who had no axe to grind and no
uneasy male dignity to defend'.

In his dealings with women Jesus was the perfect
gentleman. In today's world there are many places
where the lot of women is still extremely difficult
and where they are treated poorly. But where the

Jesus way has been adopted wholeheartedly, their situation always improves. The King who came by the Cradle Way has always made it better for the gentle hands that still rock the cradles of the world.

Prayer:
Dear Lord Jesus, thank you for your wonderful example in how we should treat each other and in particular, how we should honour womenfolk and mothers. Amen.

51

Grace or genes

(Jesus said) 'Make a tree good and its fruit will be good, or make a tree bad and its fruit will be bad, for a tree is recognized by its fruit. You brood of vipers, how can you who are evil say anything good? For out of the overflow of the heart the mouth speaks. The good man brings good things out of the good stored up in him, and the evil man brings evil things out of the evil stored up in him. But I tell you that men will have to give account on the day of judgment for every careless word they have spoken. For by your words you will be acquitted, and by your words you will be condemned.'

(Matthew 12:33–37)

•••

Some years ago *Time* magazine ran a lead article entitled 'Infidelity: It may be in our genes'. It was based on the theory of 'evolutionary psychology' which claims that human beings are not programmed for marital fidelity. In other words it is 'natural' for men and women at some time and under some circumstances to commit adultery. Fortunately the author did not say this was a wise way to act or that the 'natural' was good.

But when behaviour is explained in purely genetical terms it seems to be the thin end of the wedge. It tempts us to absolve ourselves from responsibility and accountability to God for our moral choices and behaviour. I believe that this raises several important issues for us:

- Our world view: For the Christian this is set by the Bible – God is Creator, Saviour and Final Judge. As Jesus said, God has committed all judgement to him. Not a fashionable thought in modern society but there just the same.

- Our human nature: The Bible maintains that human beings are immensely valuable to God. But it also says that we are sinful beings whose nature is flawed and weakened. Sin, whether it is infidelity, dishonesty or unkindness does indeed come 'naturally' to us.

- Our responsibility: Christians do not buy the theory $H + E = P$ (heredity plus environment equals personality). We are convinced that we are accountable to God for our actions and that this involves us in responsible daily choices.

- God's grace and forgiveness: If the bad news is that we are naturally inclined to wrong and selfish ways, then the 'tough' news is that we are all accountable to God. The good news is that God, with amazing grace, has provided for the full forgiveness of our sins and shortcomings. Jesus, as man as well as God, knows our nature; God the father, 'as a father pities his children', longs to restore us to fellowship with himself.

- Our restoration and healing: One of our good old hymns declares that we can be 'ransomed, healed, restored, forgiven'. Whether our sins are marital or parental, heterosexual or homosexual, public or private, financial or political, God holds out to us full forgiveness and the power to change for the better.

Grace, not genes, is the answer.

Prayer:
Lord help us to be honest with ourselves about our sins and failings. Please forgive and forget the past and empower us for the future. For Jesus' sake. Amen.

52

The adult exam

Remember Jesus Christ, raised from the dead, descended from David. This is my gospel, for which I am suffering even to the point of being chained like a criminal. But God's word is not chained. Therefore I endure everything for the sake of the elect, that they too may obtain the salvation that is in Christ Jesus, with eternal glory. Here is a trustworthy saying: If we died with him, we will also live with him; if we endure, we will also reign with him. If we disown him, he will also disown us; if we are faithless, he will remain faithful, for he cannot disown himself. Keep reminding them of these things. Warn them before God against quarrelling about words; it is of no value, and only ruins those who listen. Do your best to present yourself to God as one approved, a workman who does not need to be ashamed and who correctly handles the word of truth.

(2 Timothy 2:8–15)

●●●

Every now and then you come across a person who presents you with unique and life-changing challenges. One such for me thirty years ago was the late great Bishop Stephen Neill, scholar, prolific author and missionary statesman. He had an exceptional impact on me.

I was privileged to do some study under his guidance. But what I remember most about him was his concern for my basic personal life, my spiritual discipline and my relationships. Whenever I saw him after a space of time he sat me down and subjected me to a test (marked out of 20) for i. Devotion, ii. Diligence, iii. Study, iv. Priorities and v. Personal Relationships. If I got over 16 there was a grunt of approval, but below 12 earned a strong rebuke and below 9 received a verbal flagellation. For him the number of missions or conferences I was engaged in did not count if I was failing in any of the above areas of Christian discipleship.

Bishop Neill deplored the kind of preacher whose devotional life was not nourished daily by the Bible, prayer and the power of the Holy Spirit. His next two litmus tests (diligence and study) made no room for laziness and sloth. He wanted to see people who would work while others loitered, who would pray while others played, study while others slept.

The next tests (right priorities and right relationships) required a right balance between time given to work and time given to others, especially to one's spouse, family and friends. By the way, the good Bishop, whose main form of exercise was to lumber from his study to the lecture room also required me (in Oxford in 1980) to cycle 10 kilometres a day!

Oh well, perfection is boring so I won't weary you by explaining that my scores out of 20 were usually very mediocre. But I have discovered that we adults need exams just as much as our kids.

Prayer:
Lord help us to take life seriously and make the most of the precious moments that you have given us. Help us to work and worship and to give quality time to other people. Amen.

53

The tyranny of tomorrow

Who of you by worrying can add a single hour to his life ? And why do you worry about clothes? See how the lilies of the field grow. They do not labour or spin. Yet I tell you that not even Solomon in all his splendour was dressed like one of these. If that is how God clothes the grass of the field, which is here today and tomorrow is thrown into the fire, will he not much more clothe you, O you of little faith? So do not worry, saying, 'What shall we eat?' or 'What shall we drink?' or 'What shall we wear?' For the pagans run after all these things, and your heavenly Father knows that you need them. But seek first his kingdom and his righteousness, and all these things will be given to you as well. Therefore do not worry about tomorrow, for tomorrow will worry about itself. Each day has enough trouble of its own.

(Matthew 6:27–34)

●●●

People worry about many things: money, exams, marriage prospects, job opportunities, politics, the international scene. Basically all of it is anxiety about tomorrow. If the root of the problem is faithlessness, the solution for it is finding faith.

The fact is that God has so arranged things for us, his beloved creatures, that life comes to us in manageable units called 'days'. We cannot manage more than this nor can we plan for less. So we are told to pray 'give us *this* day our daily bread' so as to live not in the past or the future but in the present.

Unlike animals, we have a capacity to look to the future. The great faculty of imagination is a remarkable gift bestowed on us by our Heavenly Father. It helps us to deal positively with the future but unless it is anchored in trusting our sovereign, merciful and omnipotent God, imagination quickly runs to fear and apprehension. When that happens, the tyranny of tomorrow kills the enjoyment of today and we sentence ourselves to self-imposed prison day by day.

We can break tomorrow's despotic hold either by dying or living. For the dying person there is no tomorrow but for the truly living person this is also true. For the latter a grasp on the eternal supersedes the temporal and robs tomorrow of any corrosive power that it might have. It is not that we become careless of the future but when we put it fairly and squarely in God's hands, the next day and the next and the next disappears as a source of concern.

Jesus crammed each day full of eternity. There were hard and cruel things shaping up to assault him but it was all in his Father's loving care. His challenge to us is to be just as surely absorbed in the present as he was. Then our 'todays' become well lived and that will in turn make all our yesterdays a happy memory and all our tomorrows an exciting vision of hope.

Prayer:
Dear Heavenly Father, we lay all our past at the foot of the cross, all our tomorrows in your loving care so that we can, today, live as those who are truly alive. For Jesus' sake. Amen.

54

Knowing God

(Paul proclaimed) 'The God who made the world and everything in it is the Lord of heaven and earth and does not live in temples built by hands. And he is not served by human hands, as if he needed anything, because he himself gives all men life and breath and everything else. From one man he made every nation of men, that they should inhabit the whole earth; and he determined the times set for them and the exact places where they should live. God did this so that men would seek him and perhaps reach out for him and find him, though he is not far from each one of us. "For in him we live and move and have our being." As some of your own poets have said, "We are his offspring".

'Therefore since we are God's offspring, we should not think that the divine being is like gold or silver or stone – an image made by man's design and skill. In the past God overlooked such ignorance, but now he commands all people everywhere to repent. For he has set a day when he will judge the world with justice by the man he has appointed. He has given proof of this to all men by raising him from the dead.'

(Acts 17:24–31)

●●●

It is always exciting to visit any place that is mentioned in the Bible. For me it was a great thrill once to spend a brief time in Athens. I was immediately struck by the lingering atmosphere of Greek history and culture. The pantheon of gods, the reminders of heroes (both mythical and historical), the awesome legacy of arts – it was all still part of the scene. In the carvings you can still see the rapidly changing emotions of the heroes projected on to a supernatural world of interfering gods and goddesses all busy helping or hindering the activities of humanity. It is all part of the restless search of a religious people of a previous age.

Then there was Mars Hill. There behind and above the Temple of Jupiter is the Acropolis and the Parthenon, shrine of Athens. When Bible readers visit these places, there comes a haunting voice from the past: 'Men of Athens! I see that in every way you are very religious. For as I walked around and looked carefully at your objects of worship, I even found an altar with this inscription: TO AN UNKNOWN GOD. Now what you worship as something unknown I am going to proclaim to you.' It is the intrepid Paul, preaching to the assembled Athenian intellectuals. He had been inwardly disturbed by the fact that the city was full of idols, full of religious, philosophical and intellectual discussion. But it was all guesswork and speculation by a people bent on exploring religious novelties.

After a skilful opening in which he used local custom and a classical quote, Paul went into the attack, preaching a Jesus who could not be evaded or avoided. For Paul the unknown God had come out of the silence and shown himself in vividly observable human terms in the man Christ Jesus. And because of this, God had set a time for the universal judgement of the human race.

The reaction then, as now, was threefold: some mocked, some put it on hold so as to examine it better, some believed. Modern man's search, like the endless debates of Athens, has led into a cul-de-sac. Some people ridicule the notion that God could have come to the planet in a human form; others are not so sure and would like some help; still others have come, through an experience of the Christian faith, to know the previously unknown God. They have discovered that the truth Athens sought is not found in principles and propositions but in a person – Jesus Christ our Lord.

Prayer:
Dear God we are so grateful that, by trusting in Jesus as Saviour and Lord, we have come to know you and have found you gracious and merciful. For Jesus' sake. Amen.

55

What does your dog think?

*Whatever was to my profit I now consider loss for
the sake of Christ. What is more, I consider
everything a loss compared to the surpassing
greatness of knowing Christ Jesus my Lord, for
whose sake I have lost all things. I consider them
rubbish, that I may gain Christ and be found in him,
not having a righteousness of my own that comes
from the law, but that which is through faith in
Christ – the righteousness that comes from God and
is by faith. I want to know Christ and the power of
his resurrection and the fellowship of sharing in his
sufferings, becoming like him in his death, and so,
somehow, to attain to the resurrection from the
dead. Not that I have already obtained all this, or
have already been made perfect, but I press on to
take hold of that for which Christ Jesus took hold of
me.*

(Philippians 3:7–12)

●●●

A man once wrote to a hotel for permission to
bring his dog with him. The manager replied:

Dear Sir,
I have been in this business for 30 years. I have
never had to call the police to eject a disorderly dog. I
never had a dog set fire to a bed with a cigarette. I
have never found a hotel towel or blanket in a dog's
suitcase. Certainly your dog will be welcome …

PS if your dog will vouch for you, you may come too.

The hotel manager had obviously found a dog's nature to be more predictable and reliable than that of a human being.

The poet Matthew Arnold once divided human society into three classes: there were those, barbarians or aristocrats who had a superficial sweetness but whose chief interest in life was maintaining their privileged position; secondly, there were Philistines (for Arnold this was the middle class) who were mostly interested in money-making and religion of the most provincial kind; the third group were the lower classes who were uninhibited in their prejudices and coarse in their pleasures. Arnold's postscript was that the chief end of all three was doing whatever they liked.

The prophet Isaiah would agree with this. He said that 'every one of us has turned to his own way' or, as we say today, 'we are all doing our own thing'. It is this fatal flaw in human nature that causes all of the world's problems. Whether it is in the domestic or national scene or whether it is in the economic and industrial scene, conflict and resentment arises when human beings strive to get their own way. If I am bent on doing my own thing and you are bent on doing yours, it will not be long before we collide head on.

The good news is, of course, that Jesus Christ took on himself our human nature and, in that arena, fought with and overcame our insatiable desire to be Number One. On the cross he met and slew the egotistical poison that debilitates and eventually kills us. On the cross he took away our guilt and set us free to become the kind of human we were designed to be.

When Christ deals with your inner nature, even your dog might just vouch for you!

Prayer:
Dear Lord, I know that I am my own worst enemy and that sin and self so easily rule my thoughts and words and deeds. Thanks for Jesus and his cross. Thank you for the freedom that we enjoy. In Jesus' Name. Amen.

56

Traffic jams

We are hard pressed on every side, but not crushed; perplexed, but not in despair; persecuted, but not abandoned; struck down, but not destroyed. We always carry around in our body the death of Jesus, so that the life of Jesus may also be revealed in our body. For we who are alive are always being given over to death for Jesus' sake, so that his life may be revealed in our mortal body. So then, death is at work in us, but life is at work in you. It is written: 'I believed; therefore I have spoken.' With that same spirit of faith we also believe and therefore speak, because we know that the one who raised the Lord Jesus from the dead will also raise us with Jesus and present us with you in his presence.

(2 Corinthians 4:8–14)

●●●

Once in Cairo I was struggling to get through a horrific traffic jam to get to a speaking engagement. We were jammed in left and right and bumper to bumper. Horns were blaring, fists were being shaken and the local command of colourful speech was being exercised by infuriated taxi drivers (with the occasional pedestrian granny in black veil shouting back as good as she got).

I remember thinking that the only way I could get to my meeting would be if some superior power, like a helicopter, lifted me above the chaotic traffic jam and flew me high above the hubbub to my place of appointment. But no such force came to my aid and I had to sweat it out and prepare myself to arrive hot and flustered and half an hour late.

Life also has its traffic jams such as family mix-ups, pressures at work, financial worries, serious illness and tragedies. At such times we feel hemmed in on every side. We are blocked by different pressures, overwhelmed by all the noise of conflict and discord, crushed by anxiety and sadness. On top of all that there is the weakness and sinfulness of our own natures which can so easily trigger wrong reactions. We long for that superior force that could lift us out of the mess and enable us to cope.

The Bible, that most realistic of books, deals with our traffic jams. It speaks of two laws, 'the law of sin and death' which creates all of life's problems and 'the law of the Spirit of life in Christ Jesus' which can provide solutions (see Romans 8:2). We cannot escape from the downward drag of our own flawed natures and like gravity it exerts its constant pull on us. But like the huge jet liner that, by a superior force of aerodynamics, escapes that strong downward force, God's Spirit lifts us out of the chaos into solutions to our problems. It is not that we go up into a rarefied spiritual atmosphere free from the trials and tribulations of life. Rather, when the traffic jams hem us in, we are given the power and the wisdom to cope with them.

Prayer:
Dear Heavenly Father, you know the twists and tangles of life and of the mess we sometimes make when we try to cope with them alone. May we learn to rely more constantly on your Spirit to deal with our traffic jams. Amen.

57

The power of example

Are we beginning to commend ourselves again? Or do we need, like some people, letters of recommendation to you or from you? You yourselves are our letter, written on our hearts, known and read by everybody. You show that you are a letter from Christ, the result of our ministry, written not with ink but with the Spirit of the living God, not on tablets of stone but on tablets of human hearts. Such confidence as this is ours through Christ before God. Not that we are competent in ourselves to claim anything for ourselves, but our competence comes from God. He has made us competent as ministers of a new covenant – not of the letter but of the Spirit; for the letter kills, but the Spirit gives life.

(2 Corinthians 3:1–6)

●●●

It has been calculated that each human being profoundly influences at least 160 people during a lifetime. I do not know how this was worked out, but I am willing to believe it.

It is, of course, a very sobering thought that, whether we like it or not, we are having an impact on others for good or ill. And it is usually more by what we are than what we say. As an old Chinese proverb puts it 'one in the eye is worth two in the ear'.

I remember a scene in a film in which a father is taking his son to a movie. The boy had just turned 13 and was no longer eligible for a children's ticket. But his father boldly stepped up to the box-office and ordered one adult and one child's ticket. 'But, Dad …', said the boy, only to be silenced with a wink and a nudge from his father. As they walked into the cinema the boy looked up admiringly at his father 'Gee, Dad, I wish I could cheat as good as you!'

When I remember that scene I also remember my own father. I remember the time that I was able to hide from the conductor on the train so that he did not click my ticket. When I arrived home I gleefully told my father about how I had saved him the price of a ticket for my next journey home from school. Instead of the applause that I expected, I got the tongue-lashing of a lifetime. The fact that it is still vividly in my memory shows just how impressive was the lesson I received on financial integrity. I experienced the power of example.

Albert Schweitzer wrote: 'one thing stirs me when I look back at my youthful days, namely the fact that so many people gave me something, or were something to me without knowing it … Much that has become one's own, in gentleness, modesty, kindness, willingness to forgive, in veracity, loyalty, resignation under suffering, we owe to people in whom we have seen or experienced these values at work. If we had before us those who have thus been a blessing to us, and could tell them how it came about, they would be amazed to learn what passed from their life into ours.'

St Paul actually said that his Corinthian friends were (widely read) 'letters' from Christ. God, through his Spirit, was writing an intelligible message to others through them. So all Christians are a message to others, a powerful example by what they are as well as by what they say.

Prayer:

Lord, we are not always aware that what we are is being 'read' by others. Help us to be more alert to what you are saying to the world through our lives. For Jesus' sake. Amen.

58

God speaks

This is the message we have heard from him and declare to you: God is light; in him there is no darkness at all. If we claim to have fellowship with him yet walk in the darkness, we lie and do not live by the truth. But if we walk in the light, as he is in the light, we have fellowship with one another, and the blood of Jesus, his Son, purifies us from all sin. If we claim to be without sin, we deceive ourselves and the truth is not in us. If we confess our sins, he is faithful and just and will forgive us our sins and purify us from all unrighteousness.

(1 John 1:5–9)

●●●

At theological college we laughed at a story about a student who was seeking guidance for his future. In his room he prayed earnestly 'O, Lord, show me where you want me to go'. Another student who had entered the room to play a practical joke and was hidden in a cupboard, was unable to resist the temptation: 'Go to China!' he said. 'Thank you Lord' responded the man in prayer and to China he eventually went!!

God has spoken in strange ways. He spoke to Job out of a whirlwind, to Moses out of a burning bush and to Elijah in a 'gentle whisper'. Job was, of course, caught in a whirlwind of troubles and affliction. In his agony he did not abandon his trust in God but he did want some answers about the reason for his troubles. 'Why me?' was his anguished cry.

God had a multitude of questions from Job but at the end God put some to him that gave the whole situation a different perspective. Was he around when God laid the foundation of the earth? Did he know how God controls the weather or how he manages the instincts and impulses of the animal kingdom?

At last it dawned on Job that as a mere man he was not in a position to judge God. All the facts were not at his disposal and he had been making the mistake of assessing God by his own diminutive standard. Job repented and was restored.

There is a story told of a man in London who had been paralysed for 42 years. He lived in a small, dark room, unseen by the world at large. In order to see what was happening outside he used a large mirror held up to a window.

Perhaps in our darkness we too need a 'mirror' to get a view of a larger place. Have we looked hard enough at the Christ who reflects the glory of God in this dark world? Is our vision of God too small? Have those who are less fortunate than ourselves slipped from our view? Do we still 'see' the poor, the homeless, the sick and the oppressed?

Life is full of mystery. We ourselves are part of the mystery. The universe in all its immensity is beyond our capacity to understand and every advance in science seems to open up further puzzles. The God who made it all and holds it all together is way way beyond all the other mysteries. But thankfully at the heart of the mystery there is light, for, as the Bible says, God himself is light, a God who speaks to us out of the silence and shows himself to us so that we may have fellowship with him. Pick up a Bible and look in God's 'mirror'. You'll be glad you did.

Prayer:
Father, in the immensity of the universe we are here on this tiny planet spinning through space. Thank you for condescending to come to us in the person of Jesus. Thank you for speaking to us in your Word. Amen.

59

Mid-life doldrums

Bel bows down, Nebo stoops low; their idols are borne by beasts of burden. The images that are carried about are burdensome, a burden for the weary. They stoop and bow down together; unable to rescue the burden, they themselves go off into captivity. 'Listen to me, O house of Jacob, all you who remain of the house of Israel, you whom I have upheld since you were conceived, and have carried since your birth. Even to your old age and gray hairs I am he, I am he who will sustain you. I have made you and I will carry you; I will sustain you and I will rescue you. To whom will you compare me or count me equal? To whom will you liken me that we may be compared?'

(Isaiah 46:1–5)

•••

When my 40th birthday was approaching people said 'You'll find it a trauma'. 'Never', I said, 'not I'. But when the fateful day came it was indeed quite a trauma. Suddenly I began to think of all that I had wanted to do and all I had aimed at 20 years ago. How little I seemed to have achieved! It was depressing.

The only way I was able to recover my balance and correct my perspective was to remember that my times are in God's hands. My job is to be obedient to him day by day and leave the final outcome of my life and contribution to him.

For some people the period from about 40 to 45 is very painful and disturbing. They can feel useless and confused or else trapped by their jobs or marriages or station in life. Things get them down. Some succumb to depression and pour out their woes day and night to their spouses, bemoaning the fact that they are such failures. Sometimes people, meaning to be helpful say 'Hey, you need a change' or 'Obviously you joined the wrong company or married the wrong partner. You should quit'. All such 'helpful' advice only deepens the mid-life doldrums.

The solution? Well, faith in Christ introduces us to an eternal perspective. It rescues us from the feeling that we are compelled to get final answers or ultimate meaning in the work we do or the success we achieve. Christ's love for us does not diminish whether we are a success in the world's eyes or not. Counting our blessings is also spiritually very therapeutic. Acknowledging the good things and the good people who have come into our life is a mighty tonic. Learning to be thankful in life is the best kind of positive thinking and keeping it up is the best way to grow old gracefully.

It is also good to dream, to keep aiming higher and working towards worthy goals. If you aim for the stars you may only hit the ceiling but even that is better than no lift-off at all! So cheer up. Ronald Reagan got the US presidency when he was 70 and Nelson Mandela was even older when he became President of South Africa. And Jesus of course changed the world before he was 33. Forget about the presidency but stay with Jesus and you have a real future.

Prayer:

Dear Lord, our times are certainly in your hand and that is the safest place for them to be. So help us to quit worrying about what we amount to and instead help us to luxuriate in your love. For Jesus' sake. Amen.

60

God is Jesus' surname

But after he had considered this, an angel of the Lord appeared to him in a dream and said, 'Joseph son of David, do not be afraid to take Mary home as your wife, because what is conceived in her is from the Holy Spirit. She will give birth to a son, and you are to give him the name Jesus, because he will save his people from their sins.' All this took place to fulfill what the Lord had said through the prophet: 'The virgin will be with child and will give birth to a son, and they will call him Immanuel' – which means, 'God with us'.

(Matthew 1:20–23)

•••

When my wife and I visited Israel many years ago we stayed just outside Bethlehem. Looking out of our window it was hard to take in that this was the place where Jesus was born. But more important than the geographical location was the significance of Bethlehem as the City of David. As the angels sang on the night he was born, his birth was taking place according to prophetic promises in the Old Testament. This tiny babe was the long awaited Messiah come at last after centuries of waiting.

Part of the glad tidings of that happy day is that God is in charge of history and is in sovereign control as he moves our little planet toward its consummation in the Second Coming of Christ.

This too will take place according to prophecy just as surely as the first coming.

The angels announced him as 'this is the Saviour and he is Christ, the Lord'. And as these messengers from heaven knew, Jesus is this Christ, was the Lord, and indeed is God come in the flesh. As my daughter, Debbie, when small, once said to her mother, 'God is Jesus' surname'. Jesus himself did not suffer from any identity crisis: 'he that has seen me has seen the Father'. Jesus is therefore not simply one in a long line of religious leaders, nor one in the great pantheon of religious prophets nor a choice amid the various religious options.

The angel also said that Jesus was the Saviour. He is the Divine Rescuer and he saves us from many things: from meaninglessness, from emptiness, from loneliness, from the fear of death, from guilt and above all from the separation that has distanced us from God. Surely his coming into the world and his sacrificial death on the cross for us brings the best glad tidings of all. No wonder it made the angels sing. No wonder it makes those who trust Christ also sing. And may you also go singing and praising him from now until the end of your days.

Prayer:
Lord Jesus, Word made flesh, Saviour and King, we bow before you and praise your name. May we always worship and adore you and follow your will and way. Amen.